D0908701

Metamorphosis in Keats

THE GOTHAM LIBRARY
OF THE NEW YORK UNIVERSITY PRESS

The Gotham Library is a series of original works and critical studies published in paperback primarily for student use. The Gotham hardcover edition is primarily for use by libraries and the general reader. Devoted to significant works and major authors and to literary topics of enduring importance, Gotham Library texts offer the best in literature and criticism.

Comparative and Foreign Language Literature:
Robert J. Clements, Editor

Comparative and English Language Literature:
James W. Tuttleton, Editor

Metamorphosis in Keats

Barry Gradman

VILLA JULIE COLLEGE LIBRARY
STEVENSON, MD 21153

New York University Press · New York *and* London

PR
4838
M47G7

Copyright © 1980 by New York University

Library of Congress Cataloging in Publication Data
Gradman, Barry, 1944-
  Metamorphosis in Keats.

  (Gotham library of the New York University Press)
  Bibliography: p.
  Includes index.
  1. Keats, John, 1795-1821—Criticism and interpretation.
  2. Metamorphosis in literature.   I. Title.
PR4838.M47G7   821'.7   79-3756
ISBN 0-8147-2977-0
ISBN 0-8147-2978-9 (pbk.)

37274

Manufactured in the United States of America

For My Parents
and
Richard V. Wilson

Contents

Acknowledgments

I wish to acknowledge a large debt of thanks to Miss Aileen Ward, whose careful reading and wise criticisms of my original manuscript led me to refine my argument in a number of important ways. Her time and encouragement are deeply appreciated. I would also like to thank the administration of Swarthmore College and the Booth Ferris Foundation for a grant that enabled me to complete the manuscript during a year on leave. Part of that year was spent at the American Academy in Rome, whose gracious staff and companionable Fellows provided a delightful ambience in which to write.

Introduction

At the end of Keats's early fragment "I stood tip-toe upon a little hill," his first attempt to relate the myth of Endymion and Cynthia, there is a puzzling scene that appears to have no relation whatever to the myth itself. It is preceded by a short apostrophe to the moon-goddess: "Queen of the wide air; thou most lovely queen / Of all the brightness that mine eyes have seen!" which concludes with the poet's desideratum: "O for three words of honey, that I might / Tell but one wonder of thy bridal night!" A wonder does indeed follow:

Where distant ships do seem to show their keels,
Phoebus awhile delayed his mighty wheels,
And turned to smile upon thy bashful eyes,
Ere he his unseen pomp would solemnize.
The evening weather was so bright, and clear,
That men of health were of unusual cheer;

Stepping like Homer at the trumpet's call,
Or young Apollo on the pedestal:
And lovely women were as fair and warm,
As Venus looking sideways in alarm.
The breezes were ethereal, and pure,
And crept through half closed lattices to cure
The languid sick; it cool'd their fever'd sleep,
And soothed them into slumbers full and deep.
Soon they awoke clear eyed: nor burnt with thirsting,
Nor with hot fingers, nor with temples bursting:
And springing up, they met the wond'ring sight
Of their dear friends, nigh foolish with delight;
Who feel their arms, and breasts, and kiss and stare,
And on their placid foreheads part the hair.
Young men, and maidens at each other gaz'd
With hands held back, and motionless, amaz'd
To see the brightness in each other's eyes;
And so they stood, fill'd with a sweet surprise,
Until their tongues were loos'd in poesy.
Therefore no lover did of anguish die:
But the soft numbers, in that moment spoken,
Made silken ties, that never may be broken.
Cynthia! I cannot tell the greater blisses,
That follow'd thine, and thy dear shepherd's kisses:
Was there a Poet born?—but now no more,
My wand'ring spirit must no further soar.[1]

Here the fragment ends. Apparently the curing of the languid sick
and their union with men of health and lovely women is intended
to celebrate the uniting of Cynthia and Endymion, though why
precisely a scene of reanimation, of metamorphosis from sickness to
health, should be appropriate is not made clear. Moreover, Keats
seems willingly to have defeated his narrative endeavor by beginning with the myth's climactic event. Indeed, the poem's concluding vague question and Keats's suppression of his "wand'ring
spirit" indicate that he does not yet realize what the Endymion
myth might be made to signify. Yet one feels that something
deeply felt has been expressed in these lines. The curing of the sick

lovers, however obscure its relation to the Cynthia and Endymion myth, has a dramatic energy not evident elsewhere in "I stood tip-toe." Indeed, the scene's anomalous appearance suggests that it is satisfying some pressing but unrecognized impulse of the poet's imagination, an impulse that has something to do with the attainment of erotic felicity and the vanquishing of death. The achievement of these desires is described by an incident of metamorphosis so wondrous that once the languid sick are transformed into healthy lovers, nothing more can be—and perhaps need be—said.

The episode begins at twilight, a time of transition. Keats creates a suspensive, anticipatory mood by having the declining sun-god pause as the moon is about to rise: "Phoebus awhile delayed his mighty wheels, / And turned to smile upon thy bashful eyes, / Ere he his unseen pomp would solemnize." He then juxtaposes health and disease. Heroic men and aroused women ("as fair and warm, / As Venus looking sideways in alarm") delight in the refreshing weather whose "ethereal and pure" breezes are the very agents of health, for they penetrate the half-closed lattices of sick-rooms and transform the "fever'd sleep" of the sick to a curing slumber. They awake restored: "clear eyed: nor burnt with thirsting, / Nor with hot fingers, nor with temples bursting." This transformation is followed by the joining of the two groups, those never ill and those just cured, in "amaz'd" rejoicing. Significantly, the united lovers' joy is sealed by their speaking in verse:

... their tongues were loos'd in poesy.
Therefore no lover did of anguish die:
But the soft numbers, in that moment spoken.
Made silken ties, that never may be broken.

Metamorphosis defeats morbid "anguish"; the celebration of its triumph is poetry.

This curiously forceful conclusion to "I stood tip-toe" is noteworthy because it adumbrates, in a condensed, inchoate way, similar metamorphic episodes that recur throughout Keats's poetry. Paradigmatically, the experience of the sick lovers consists of three distinct stages: illness, slumber, health. This is the earliest manifestation of what I should like to call a three-part "metamorphosis pattern," discernible in a number of Keats's subsequent poems in which it serves to express a wide spectrum of the poet's moral and aesthetic attitudes. Time and again we are confronted with a character in a narrative poem or the speaker of a lyric who is in what can be generally termed a state of discontent, of spiritual "sickness." This may be variously manifested as intense erotic longing, as physical withering, as painful ignorance, as a radical disturbance of the senses symbolizing a spiritual confusion ("My heart aches, and a drowsy numbness pains / My sense . . ."). This state of discontent is then followed by some sort of lapse of ordinary consciousness: a sleep, a swoon, a paroxysm, a sexual climax, a morbid introspectiveness, a deep chill. All of these lapses are deathlike; that is, they are metaphors for dying, and in some the morbidity is made explicit. They are then followed by the rising to a new life or to a renovated consciousness, and frequently this acquisition of new life or consciousness is accompanied by images of flight, either upward or outward. The end of the metamorphic process varies significantly from poem to poem and is a measure of Keats's moral and aesthetic stance at any given point in his development.

Sometimes the metamorphosis pattern gives form to climactic episodes in Keats's verse (as in *Endymion,* both *Hyperion* fragments, *Lamia),* while at other times it structures entire poems *(The Eve of St. Agnes,* "Ode to a Nightingale"). In many ways its clearest expression occurs at the end of Book III of *Hyperion,* in which Apollo endures a severe physical and psychic ordeal whereby he "Die[s] into life"; elsewhere the metamorphoses are more covert, but the pattern outlined above can always be seen as ordering the narrative or lyric particulars. It is, of course, impossible to say whether or not Keats was aware of the recurrence of such a design in his work, but in the long run this does not matter. The important considerations are why it appears so frequently and what artistic purposes it comes to serve.

In her discussion of *The Fall of Hyperion,* Aileen Ward cites an essay by Yeats in which the poet speaks of the " 'one scene, one adventure, one picture' " . . . "the image of a man's secret life, which, 'if he would but brood over it his life long,' would bring him in the end to an understanding of all his experience." For Ward, the face of Moneta, goddess of tragic vision, is "the ultimate image of Keats's poetry":

It is the very foundation of Keats's poetic structure, the metamorphoses recurrent throughout his poetry of the "Beauty
that must die" and the dead miraculously brought to life
again; it suggests the driving force behind the metamorphoses
of his own identity.[2]

These suggestive remarks have led me to explore the idea of metamorphosis in Keats's poetry, for I believe that it corresponds to
what Yeats further calls "the one Myth for every man, which, if we
but knew it, would make us understand all he did and thought." [3]
Metamorphosis, to be sure, does not tell us everything, but it is, as
I hope to prove, a primary impulse of Keats's art, one of his principal means of articulation. In the following pages I shall examine
how metamorphosis figures as both a principle of form and a
bearer of meaning in most of Keats's major poems. On the basis of
these examinations, I shall speculate in the epilogue as to why
episodes of metamorphosis recur so frequently in his work; that is,
I shall address myself to the psychological needs that its repetition
is satisfying.

Finally, I must mention here an essay on Keats's narrative
poems by Miriam Allott, in which she discerns "a patterned sequence of images possessing a force and frequency peculiar to
[Keats]," whereby the poet expresses his attitude toward the relationship between the ideal and the actual. "The frequent recurrence of this pattern," she continues, "makes us realize that Keats's
verse, though unequal and fragmentary in effect, betrays the driving compulsion of the genuine artist." Specifically, this patterned
sequence of images, or "emotional curve," is evident in episodes of
"a lover falling into an enchantment, enjoying every kind of sensuous delight while it lasts, and then awakening to unpleasant
reality." [4] The emotional curve that Allott discusses is similar to
what I am calling the Keatsian metamorphosis pattern; that is, I
believe we are responding to the same phenomenon in the poet's
work. But my description of it differs from hers in several important ways. Allott is describing what might be termed negative metamorphosis—a change for the worse, such as that which befalls the
knight at arms in "La Belle Dame Sans Merci" or Endymion in his
various encounters with the moon-goddess. But Endymion's awak-
enings to unpleasant reality are all temporary; ultimately he is

immortalized, somewhat unconvincingly, to be sure, but the over-all design of the poem is to award Endymion the otherworldly happiness he has presumably earned. The knight's experience is indeed a genuinely negative transformation, but "La Belle Dame Sans Merci" for that very reason strikes me as an exception. Almost everywhere else in Keats's poetry, metamorphosis is positive because it yields either a higher state of being or a more refined, though often burdened, awareness. But the knight learns nothing from his encounter with La Belle Dame; to the bewildered "O what can ail thee, knight at arms" he can offer no explanation, but merely an assertion of his debility. Finally, there is *Lamia,* in which the metamorphoses do indeed seem to be negative; but, as I hope to demonstrate, in that poem Keats is parodying his own customary procedure. Still, Allott's essay has fostered my own thinking about Keatsian metamorphosis, and I am indebted to many of its insights.

II. Metamorphosis and the Creative Process

The idea of metamorphosis is also implicit in Keats's conception of how the imagination creates poetry, insofar as one can piece together a conception from his spontaneous comments on the poetic process in his letters. For while Keats surely had ideas about art, he was of course in no sense a theorist, and his ideas were qualified and altered in important ways as his career evolved.

Keats consistently expressed his aesthetic ideas through metaphor and analogy. In an early letter to Benjamin Bailey, he states that he is "certain of nothing but of the holiness of the Heart's affections and the truth of Imagination," whose operation he then illustrates with the famous allusion to Milton: "The Imagination may be compared to Adam's dream: he awoke and found it truth." [5] It is worth investigating the scene in Book VIII of *Paradise Lost* to which Keats is alluding to see precisely how it illustrates his understanding of the imaginative process. Interestingly, the Miltonic passage has certain features in common with the conclusion to "I stood tip-toe," features that correspond to the three-part metamorphosis pattern. First, Adam recounts to Raphael how he was

"Dazzl'd, and spent, sunk down" from having engaged with God in "celestial Colloquy sublime." [6] To refresh himself, he "sought repair / Of sleep," during which God closed his eyes "but op'n left the Cell / Of Fancy my internal sight . . ." (VIII, 457-58, 460-61). In the dream God removes Adam's rib, which "he form'd and fashion'd with his hands" into a Creature

> so lovely fair
> That what seem'd fair in all the World, seem'd now
> Mean, or in her summ'd up, in her contain'd
> And in her looks, which from that time infus'd
> Sweetness into my heart, unfelt before,
> And into all things from her Air inspir'd,
> The spirit of love and amorous delight.
>
> (VIII, 469, 471-77)

Adam then awakes, to find his dream become truth. The creation of Eve involves a double metamorphosis: Adam's rib is formed and fashioned into his "heart's desire" (VII, 451), whereupon Adam's awareness is itself radically transformed: what seemed fair before is now mean compared to Eve, whose sweetness, "unfelt before," now infuses all his being. The passage's numerous temporal indicators, as well as Milton's narrative technique, make clear how Adam's experience progresses in clearly defined stages, a sequence that Keats must have found congenial.

In comparing the imagination to Adam's dream, then, Keats indicates that the artist does not merely reflect reality but, rather, transmutes it. This notion is borne out by the metaphoric language that Keats habitually uses to describe the creative process. For example, in another early letter, to the painter Benjamin Robert Haydon, Keats speaks of "looking upon the Sun the Moon the Stars, the Earth and its contents as materials to form greater things—that is to say ethereal things . . ." (I, 143). The important words are "materials" and "ethereal." As Stuart Sperry has very ably pointed out, " 'etherealization,' or the way in which material forms are 'put into etherial existence,' is close to the heart of [Keats's] notion of poetic creativity." [7] Sperry argues convincingly that the meaning of "ethereal" for Keats may be determined by examining its usage as a term in chemistry. Indeed, he points out

> how many of Keats's favorite words for referring to poetry or the process by which it is created—"abstract" and "abstraction," "spirit" and "spiritual," "essence" and "essential," "intense" and "intensity," "distill" and "distillation," "empyreal," "ethereal," "sublime"—all have more or less exact meanings in the chemistry of his day.[8]

Having become familiar with this language in his medical training, Keats recognized (however unconsciously) that "certain fundamental analogies between the laws of physical change and the processes of the imagination were current and readily available in the chemical theory of his day," and he exploited their expressive possibilities.[9]

In short, the central point of all Keats's early observations on the poetic process is that nature and human experience are "materials," which the poetic imagination "transforms . . . to a *higher* state, akin to the 'ethereal.' "[10] But Sperry is right to stress that Keat's "ethereal" and its synonyms do not mean "transcendental." Keats's natural world is not at all Blake's "Vala," a corrupt, delusive covering of true reality, which the imagination must penetrate beyond. Sense experience always remains the sine qua non for Keats and is not overwhelmed by the imagination but, rather, refined and transmuted by the intensity of its creative power.

The artist's refinement, however, is clearly of a more exalted nature than the materials upon which it is based. That the imagination metamorphoses nature and experience from a lower to a higher state is implicit in all of Keats's comments on the creative process that employ chemical metaphors, just as it is central to Milton's lines on Adam's dream. Eve's beauty is so elevated that it reduces what seemed fair in all the world to meanness, or else is the sublime epitome of what preceded her ("or in her summ'd up, in her contain'd"); similarly, not only Adam, but all things are "inspir'd" by "The spirit of love and amorous delight" she radiates.

I stress this movement from the natural and fundamental to the exalted and ethereal in Keats's spontaneous descriptions of the creative process because a similar upward movement, physical or metaphorical or both, is more or less explicit in those poems that follow the metamorphosis pattern. Thus when in "I stood tip-toe" the languid sick are wondrously transformed to energetic lovers, Keats describes them as "springing up" after they have been cured (227). In subsequent poems, a mortal shepherd will be "ensky'd," an ignorant deity will be raised to comprehending godhood, a naïve girl will rise from her bed an experienced woman and take flight with her lover into the storm outside, a listener's spirit will soar toward the nightingale (which subsequently flies away), a dreamer will mount a stairway and become a poet.

Notes

1. "I stood tip-toe," 205-6, 209-10, 211-42. All quotations of Keats's poetry are from *The Poems of John Keats,* ed. Jack Stillinger (Cambridge, Mass.: Harvard Univ. Press, 1978). Line numbers are hereafter included in parentheses in the text.
2. Aileen Ward, *John Keats: The Making of a Poet* (New York: Viking Press, 1963), p. 340.
3. W. B. Yeats, "At Stratford-on-Avon," in *Essays and Introductions* (New York: Macmillan, 1961), p. 107.
4. Miriam Allott, " 'Isabella,' 'The Eve of St. Agnes,' and 'Lamia,' " in *John Keats: A Reassessment,* ed. Kenneth Muir (Liverpool: Liverpool Univ. Press, 1958), p. 47.
5. *The Letters of John Keats, 1814-1821,* ed. Hyder E. Rollins, 2 vols. (Cambridge, Mass.: Harvard Univ. Press, 1958), I, 185. References by volume and page number to this edition are hereafter included in parentheses in the text.
6. *John Milton: Complete Poems and Major Prose,* ed. Merritt Y. Hughes (New York: Odyssey Press, 1957), p. 373, lines 457, 455. Additional references by book and line number are given in the text.
7. Stuart M. Sperry, *Keats the Poet* (Princeton: Princeton Univ. Press, 1973), p. 35. See chap. 2, "The Chemistry of the Poetic Process."
8. Ibid., p. 37. Sperry notes: "It would be wrong to argue that the analogies by which Keats regularly visualizes the imagination and its operations ever constituted a coherent, fully developed theory. He himself nowhere provided so detailed or abstract an analysis of the poetic process, nor is there any reason to imagine he ever attempted to formulate such a conception in any deliberate way. His sense of artistic creativity was partly subliminal and largely metaphoric. Nevertheless, there emerges in his letters of the winter of 1817-1818, when he was revising *Endymion* for the press, a series of comments on

the subject of the imagination that organize themselves around the chemical metaphor with such consistency as to justify one's speaking of an early conception of the poetic process" (pp. 49-50).

9. The contemporary chemist on whom Sperry most relies is Sir Humphry Davy, since Davy himself drew explicit analogies between the workings of science and art. "The forms and appearances of the beings and substances of the external world are almost infinitely various, and they are in a state of continued alteration: the whole surface of the earth even undergoes modifications," wrote Davy. Indeed, "a series of decompositions and recombinations are constantly occurring in the phenomena of nature, and in the operations of art," whereby "one variety of matter becomes as it were transmuted into another." Davy's notion of "decompositions and recombinations" also appears in the critical discourse of William Hazlitt, the contemporary critic who most influenced Keats. Hazlitt wrote that "In Chaucer we perceive a fixed essence of character. In Shakespeare there is a continual composition and decomposition of its elements, a fermentation of every particle in the whole mass, by its alternate affinity or antipathy to other principles which are brought into contact with it." And Keats in turn echoes Hazlitt in another letter to Haydon, where he refers to "The innumerable compositions and decompositions which take place between the intellect and its thousand materials before it arrives at that trembling delicate and snail-horn perception of Beauty" (I, 265). Sperry notes these comparisons and others in his second chapter; see *Keats the Poet*, pp. 41-42ff.

10. Ibid., p. 47, italics added.

1.

Early Verse: The Most Heart-easing
Things

The travail of incessant rebirth was never far away from him;
he was forever passing beyond despair.
—John Middleton Murry, *Keats and Shakespeare*

The curing of the sick lovers at the end of "I stood tip-toe"
clearly reflects (perhaps as wish-fulfillment) Keats's medical training in the wards of Guy's Hospital, and it is interesting to note how
often in his early verse the effect of poetry, upon both writer and
reader, is said to be one of *healing*.[1] This is how the notion of
metamorphosis is most often expressed in Keats's early writing.
Though none of the poems in his 1817 volume follows the three-
part metamorphosis pattern, we can discern throughout these early
works a preoccupation with curative, renovating change, which, in
Endymion will become a principle of structure.

For example, Keats asserts in "Sleep and Poetry" that "the great
end / Of poesy" is "that it should be a friend / To sooth the cares,
and lift the thoughts of man" (245-47). Keats never really abandoned this idea; the Keatsian persona in *The Fall of Hyperion* affirms

1

poetry's power to medicine the diseased spirit when he proclaims
" 'sure a poet is a sage; / A humanist, physician to all men' " (I,
189-90). Thus, while it is tempting to read the poetry Keats wrote
before *Endymion* as an unshadowed romp in the bower-realm of
"Flora, and old Pan," in fact Keatsian delight is a victory (in these
poems more asserted than earned) over what he referred to in an
early letter to Haydon as his "horrid Morbidity of Temperament
which has shown itself at intervals—it is I have no doubt the greatest Enemy and stumbling block I have to fear" (I, 142). Indeed,
though it is not much noted, Keats is the most morbid of the major
English Romantics, more so than Byron, whose air of fatality is
more often than not a self-dramatizing device, one of many poetic
ploys. But Keats's grief at the deaths of his parents and other
family members at crucial points in his emotional development
profoundly shadowed his spirit and made him fear his own early
demise.[2] In the same letter to Haydon, Keats begins by quoting
the opening lines of *Love's Labour's Lost,* which describe how Fame
"will grace us in the disgrace of death":

> When spite of cormorant devouring time
> The endeavor of this present breath may buy
> That Honor which shall bate his Scythe's keen edge
> And make us heirs of all eternity.
>
> (I, 141)

He is twenty-one, but tells Haydon, "It cannot be long first the
endeavor of this present breath will soon be over" (I, 141). "I am
extremely glad that a time must come when every thing will leave
not a wrack behind" (I, 142). When he is not brooding on his
death, he complains of brain-sickness: "I cannot write while my
spirit is fevered in a contrary direction . . ." (I, 142). But, characteristically, he proclaims that even a horrid morbidity of temperament has assets as well as liabilities: "every ill has its share of
good—this very bane would at any time enable me to look with an
obstinate eye on the Devil Himself" (I, 142). It is precisely this
heroic obstinacy to outface difficulty and death that motivates
Keats's poetry from start to finish. The attempt will take many
forms; in the early verse it appears in his frequently asserted belief

that poetry should "simply tell the most heart-easing things" ("Sleep and Poetry," 268).

What most eases the heart, and therefore inspires the poet, is the beauty of nature. "For what has made the sage or poet write / But the fair paradise of Nature's light?" ("I stood tip-toe," 125-26). Flora's delight "Charms us at once away from all our troubles: / So that we feel uplifted from the world" (138-39). Nature in the early Keats is typically "Some flowery spot, sequester'd, wild, romantic" ("To George Felton Mathew," 37), a bower that soothes and refreshes the spirit. This notion is most fully expressed in the opening to Book I of *Endymion*, near in mood to the preceding verse, where all beautiful things—both natural delights and the poetry celebrating them—are said to "keep / A bower quiet for us, and a sleep / Full of sweet dreams, and health, and quiet breathing" (I, 3-5). Beauty is eternal, and Keats tells us why we must always have it:

> Spite of despondence, of the inhuman dearth
> Of noble natures, of the gloomy days,
> Of all the unhealthy and o'er-darkened ways
> Made for our searching: yes, in spite of all,
> Some shape of beauty moves away the pall
> From our dark spirits. Such the sun, the moon,
> Trees old, and young sprouting a shady boon
> For simple sheep; and such are daffodils
> With the green world they live in . . .
> All lovely tales that we have heard or read:
> An endless fountain of immortal drink,
> Pouring unto us from the heaven's brink.
>
> (I, 8-16)

Beauty in all its forms revitalizes the despondent spirit, casting "a cheering light" (I, 30) on the unhealthy and o'er-darkened ways of human existence. Things of beauty "always must be with us, *or we die*" (I, 33; italics added).

Often in his early verse Keats celebrates the refreshing power of nature without referring to any sort of discontent to be assuaged by it, which results in a poetry whose forward movement can only be sustained by the piling up of images, as in the fragmentary and directionless "Calidore":

> Young Calidore is paddling o'er the lake;
> His healthful spirit eager and awake
> To feel the beauty of a silent eve,
> Which seem'd full loath this happy world to leave;
> The light dwelt o'er the scene so lingeringly.
> He bares his forehead to the cool blue sky,
> And smiles at the far clearness all around,
> Until his heart is well nigh over wound,
> And turns for calmness to the pleasant green
> Of easy slopes, and shadowy trees that lean
> So elegantly o'er the waters' brim
> And show their blossoms trim.[3]
>
> (1-12)

But this sort of pure description is relatively infrequent in the early Keats; more typical is his very first poem, the "Imitation of Spenser." The first two stanzas dazzle with images of light, but in the third Keats briefly mentions the spirit's shadows, which that brightness may mitigate:

> Ah! could I tell the wonders of an isle
> That in that fairest lake had placed been,
> I could e'en Dido of her grief beguile,
> Or rob from aged Lear his bitter teen:
> For sure so fair a place was never seen,
> Of all that ever charm'd romantic eye:
> It seem'd an emerald in the silver sheen
> Of the bright waters; or as when on high,
> Through clouds of fleecy white, laughs the coerulean sky.

It is Keats's *telling* that would provide the curative effect, and the allusions to Dido and Lear signify the intensity of Keats's early faith in poetry's power to heal.

This faith is prevalent throughout the early verse. In his sonnet

"To My Brothers," Keats describes a comfortable domestic scene: "And while, for rhymes, I search around the poles, / Your eyes are fix'd, as in poetic sleep, / Upon the lore so voluble and deep, / That aye at fall of night our care condoles" (5-8). Anticipating the conflict in *The Fall of Hyperion* between poetry writing and socially useful work, Keats's verse-letter "To My Brother George" records a pang of guilt at his "mad ambition"; he would be "dearer to society" if he could "smother" it. Poetry, however, clearly has the higher claim, for as he ingenuously notes,

> At times, 'tis true, I've felt relief from pain
> When some bright thought has darted through my brain:
> Through all that day I've felt a greater pleasure
> Than if I'd brought to light a hidden treasure.
> As to my sonnets, though none else should heed them,
> I feel delighted, still, that you should read them.
> Of late, too, I have had much calm enjoyment,
> Stretch'd on the grass at my best lov'd employment
> Of scribbling lines for you. These things I thought
> While, in my face, the freshest breeze I caught.
> E'en now I'm pillowed on a bed of flowers. . . .
>
> (113-23)

Yearning for nature, Keats asks in "To one who has been long in city pent":

> Who is more happy, when, with heart's content,
>   Fatigued he sinks into some pleasant lair
>   Of wavy grass, and reads a debonair
> And gentle tale of love and languishment?
>
> (5-8)

The same contrast between urban imprisonment and the bowery world of verse structures Keats's sonnet "Written on the Day that Mr. Leigh Hunt left Prison." It is poetry that has transformed Hunt's cell into a spiritual bower, making his immortal spirit "as free / As the sky-searching lark, and as elate":

In Spenser's halls he strayed, and bowers fair,
   Culling enchanted flowers; and he flew
With daring Milton through the fields of air:
   To regions of his own his genius true
Took happy flights.[4]

                          (9-13)

Even when nature herself fails to soothe, as in "Keen, fitful gusts are whisp'ring here and there," the memory of the genial warmth of poetry reading comforts:

Yet feel I little of the cool bleak air,
   Or of the dead leaves rustling drearily,
   Or of those silver lamps that burn on high,
Or of the distance from home's pleasant lair.
For I am brimfull of the friendliness
   That in a little cottage I have found;
Of fair-hair'd Milton's eloquent distress,
   And all his love for gentle Lycid drown'd;
Of lovely Laura in her light green dress,
   And faithful Petrarch gloriously crown'd.

                          (5-14)

In its geniality, poetry is transformative. Milton's grief for his friend is made beautiful by his eloquent praise, as is Laura by her verdant dress and Petrarch by his laurel. And Keats's convivial memory of them changes physical discomfort to spirtual ease.

The idea of metamorphosis becomes explicit in Keats's verse-letter "To George Felton Mathew," a fellow poet whose saccharine aestheticism Keats then found congenial, though he was soon to outgrow it. He begins by asserting once again poetry's essentially curative power: the thought of another poetic partnership, that of Beaumont and Fletcher, "diffuses / Over the genius loving heart, a feeling / Of all that's high, and great, and good, and healing" (8-10). The verse-letter proceeds in desultory fashion for about seventy lines; but in the last verse-paragraph there is a significant inventive touch:

For thou wast once a flowerest blooming wild,
Close to the source, bright, pure, and undefil'd,
Whence gush the streams of song: in happy hour
Came chaste Diana from her shady bower,
Just as the sun was from the east uprising;
And, as for him some gift she was devising,
Beheld thee, pluck'd thee, cast thee in the stream
To meet her glorious brother's greeting beam.
I marvel much that thou has never told
How, from a flower, into a fish of gold
Apollo chang'd thee; how thou next didst seem
A black-eyed swan upon the widening stream;
And when thou first didst in that mirror trace
The placid features of a human face:
That thou hast never told thy travels strange,
And all the wonders of the mazy range
O'er pebbly crystal, and o'er golden sands;
Kissing thy daily food from Naiad's pearly hands.
(76-93)

The literal starting point of this series of Ovidian metamorphoses (which clearly adumbrate those of *Endymion*) is "the source, bright, pure, and undefiled, / Whence gush the streams of song," that is, the Helicon springs, home of the Muses. Significantly, Mathew's fanciful transformations occur just as the sun rises; many of the subsequent metamorphoses in Keats's poetry will occur at the transitional hours of dawn or sunset. Keats's elaborate compliment to Mathew thus expresses, however obliquely, the one aesthetic tenet that underlies all his early verse, namely, that poetry both originates in and proceeds from the imagination's power to metamorphose reality, variously imaged as the transition from discomfort to ease, from spiritual discontent to health.

Toward the end of 1819, Keats felt secure enough in his role as poet to compose an aesthetic credo, "Sleep and Poetry," in the course of which he outlined a poetic program for the years to come. Unfortunately, the poem's argument is not altogether cogent, for there appears to be an unresolved contradiction between his reiterated general conception of poetry as refreshing and curative and his description of the kind of poetry he feels obliged to write in the future. But this inconsistency is revealing, for it reconfirms the intensity of Keats's current faith in poetry's essentially healing power.

The aesthetic program appears to have two stages. The first, corresponding to the kind of verse he has so far written, is a simple celebration of nature's pure and soothing beauty, the realm of "Flora, and old Pan," where the poet can "sleep in the grass, / Feed upon apples red, and strawberries, / And choose each pleasure that my fancy sees" (102-4). The second stage, one of serious moral commitment, is more ambiguously imaged:

> And can I ever bid these joys farewell?
> Yes, I must pass them for a nobler life,
> Where I may find the agonies, the strife
> Of human hearts: for lo! I see afar,
> O'er sailing the blue cragginess, a car
> And steeds with streamy manes—the charioteer
> Looks out upon the winds with glorious fear:
>
> (122-28)

He knows that the exclusively sensuous, pagan bower-world must be passed over for a poetry that confronts the human tragedy; the difficulty, however, is that Keats's subsequent vision of the charioteer seems not to serve its intended purpose of emblemizing such a poetry. Something seems to be blocking the appropriate images of struggle and torment:

> The charioteer with wond'rous gesture talks
> To the trees and mountains; and there soon appear
> Shapes of delight, of mystery, and fear,
> Passing along before a dusky space
> Made by some mighty oaks: as they would chase
> Some ever-fleeting music on they sweep.
> Lo! how they murmur, laugh, and smile, and weep:
> Some with upholden hand and mouth severe;
> Some with their faces muffled to the ear
> Between their arms; some, clear in youthful bloom,

Go glad and smilingly athwart the gloom;
Some looking back, and some with upward gaze;
Yes, thousands in a thousand different ways
Flit onward—now a lovely wreath of girls
Dancing their sleek hair into tangled curls;
And now broad wings. Most awfully intent,
The driver of those steeds is forward bent,
And seems to listen: O that I might know
All that he writes with such a hurrying glow.
                              (136-54)

Keats's friend Richard Woodhouse assumed that "the agonies, the strife / of human hearts" referred to epic poetry and that the charioteer is a "personification of the Epic poet, when the enthusiasm of inspiration is upon him . . ." [5] This seems doubtful, since the charioteer's conjuring of nature produces "shapes of delight" that seem more at home in a visionary allegory or romance than in a poem of martial struggle and personal conflict. But even if Woodhouse is right, the passage is contradictory:

The visions are all fled—the car is fled
Into the light of heaven, and in their stead
A sense of real things comes doubly strong,
And, like a muddy stream, would bear along
My soul to nothingness: but I will strive
Against all doubtings, and will keep alive
The thought of that same chariot, and the strange
Journey it went.
                              (155-62)

If the dark reality of human hearts is the sought-after goal, why is the vision's evanescence *followed* by "a sense of real things," which is clearly pejorative—"like a muddy stream" leading the soul to nothingness? This confusion, I would suggest, is due in part to Keats's strong attachment to Flora's realm, which he does not want to abandon because of its proven power to soothe and heal the discontented spirit. The ambitions of his mind and the promptings of his heart are not now congruent, as they will be later on in his career. It is hindsight that encourages us to view the poetic program outlined in "Sleep and Poetry," despite its inchoate expression, as adumbrating similar projections in his letters, such as the famous simile of human life as "a large Mansion of Many Apartments," whose first chamber is "infant or thoughtless," but whose second, though filled with "pleasant wonders," eventually has the effect of "sharpening one's vision into the heart and nature of Man—of convincing ones nerves that the world is full of Misery and Heartbreak, Pain, Sickness and oppression . . ." (I, 280-81).

Thus it is Keats's allegiance to Flora's realm that causes him temporarily to suppress "the agonies, the strife / Of human hearts" and simply to reassert poetry's restorative power. "Sleep and Poetry" is filled with such reassertions. "A drainless shower / Of light is poesy" (235-36); ". . . it should be a friend / To sooth the cares, and lift the thoughts of man" (246-47); for "they shall be accounted poet kings / Who simply tell the most heart-easing things" (267-68). These sentiments determine his critique of the "strange potency" of recent works by Byron (and possibly Coleridge's *Christabel),* whose subjects "Are ugly clubs, the poets Polyphemes / Disturbing the grand sea" (234-35). He acknowledges poetry's claim to effects of majesty—" 'Tis might half slumb'ring on its own right arm" (237), but says its power should derive from the enchantment of language, not merely from subjects that are intrinsically provocative—"Darkness, and worms, and shrouds, and sepulcres," "the burrs, / And thorns of life" (243-45). However accurate a criticism this may be of the works Keats had in mind, it indicates his current predisposition to avoid poetry that dwells upon human discontents and to favor that which soothes and heals.

But it is not only the realm of Flora and old Pan that can soothe and heal the discontented spirit. The heart may also be eased by dwelling in a visionary realm, like that of the charioteer, where there are no muddy streams to bear the soul to nothingness. Indeed, it is the absence of the particulars of human agony—"The weariness, the fever, and the fret," as Keats would describe it in the "Nightingale" ode—that characterizes both Flora's and the charioteer's realm and that joined them in Keats's mind. To reach and dwell in a visionary world is to elevate the spirit to a perception of beauty and peace unclouded by skepticism or "dis-ease." The curing of the sick lovers in "I stood tip-toe" may thus be seen as expressing Keats's desire to attain such a state; the episode symbolizes the imagination's longing for visionary awareness. Similarly, the lovers' speaking in poesy once their healing has been effected signals Keats's desire to set his forthcoming verse in a world of vision. The concluding lines to the charioteer passage in "Sleep and Poetry" state rhetorically what the magical transformation at the close of "I stood tip-toe" expresses symbolically. For when the charioteer's conjured "shapes of delight" vanish, and his "car is fled / Into the light of heaven," Keats vows that he

> will strive
> Against all doubtings, and will keep alive
> The thought of that same chariot, and the strange
> Journey it went.

The thought is kept alive in *Endymion,* a poem of strange journeys, not only for the shepherd-prince of Latmos, but for his creator as well. For Keats will discover in the course of his long poetic odyssey that the visionary realm, despite its prodigious allure, cannot by itself encompass his maturing apprehension of the truth of human experience. He will discover that poetry cannot *"simply* tell the most heart-easing things."

Notes

1. For details of Keats's experience at Guy's Hospital, see W. J. Bate, *John Keats* (New York: Oxford Univ. Press, 1966), pp. 44ff.
2. See Aileen Ward, *John Keats: The Making of a Poet* (New York: Viking Press, 1963), pp. 9-11.
3. "Calidore," as its Spenserian title indicates, is one of Keats's early attempts to set a poem in a medieval ambience, although he was unable to develop the world of chivalry in any significant way at this time. It figures in "To Mary Frogley," "Woman! when I behold thee flippant, vain," and is referred to briefly in the verse-letters "To My Brother George" (17-18, 26ff.) and "To Charles Cowden Clarke" (46-47). An important clue to Keats's interest in the medieval world is contained in the "Specimen of an Induction to a Poem"

(the poem is "Calidore"), which begins, "Lo! I must tell a tale of chivalry" and then proceeds to ask, "then how shall I / Revive the dying tones of minstrelsy, / Which linger yet about lone gothic arches, / In dark green ivy, and among wild larches?" (31-34). Keats's early medievalism was an attempt to revitalize a moribund tradition; but it was the world of Greek myth, not that of chivalry, that he ultimately decided to "revive."

4. Hunt actually converted his prison quarters into a scholar's bower. Ward notes that his cell was "papered with trellised roses and furnished with bookcases, busts of his favourite poets, and a piano. . . . Venetian blinds hid the bars of his window, the prison yard outside was planted with pansies and sweetbriar, and the ceiling of his living room was painted with a blue sky and fleecy clouds" (*John Keats: The Making of a Poet*, p. 36).

5. Stuart M. Sperry, Jr., "Richard Woodhouse's Interleaved and Annotated Copy of Keats's Poems (1817)," *Literary Monographs* 1, ed. E. Rothstein and T. K. Denseath (1967), p. 154.

2.

Endymion: Tortured with Renewed Life

The Endymion myth, which tells of a mortal shepherd who wins the love of the moon-goddess and is immortalized, is obviously a fitting frame in which Keats could picture and—as it turned out—question the visionary world as an emblem of human aspiration and fulfillment. We have noted that "I stood tip-toe" (which Keats originally referred to as "Endymion" [I, 121] was a first, aborted attempt to recount the myth; toward the end of that poem Keats indicates its visionary potential. The aesthetic effect of this "sweetest of all songs" is said to be "aye refreshing," bringing "Shapes from the invisible world, unearthly signing / From out the middle air . . ." (182, 183, 186-87). Inherent in Keats's fanciful account of how the myth's progenitor was inspired by the beautiful but desolate moon in her "starry dwelling" (198) is an upward movement from the earthbound to the heavenly:

Ah! surely he had burst our mortal bars;
Into some wond'rous region he had gone,
To search for thee, divine Endymion!
                    (190-92)

To dwell in such a "refreshing" region, as poet or reader, is to experience an imaginative transmutation from mundane consciousness to a new, "wond'rous" state of being.

The Endymion myth is essentially one of metamorphosis: a mortal is transformed, through a goddess's love for him, into an immortal. The dénouement of the tale clearly implies a preference for the "invisible world" over ordinary life with its inevitable dissatisfactions and inadequacies, from which the mortal shepherd is literally distracted—drawn away—by the moon-goddess's love for him. Keats's challenge, in adapting the Endymion myth to illustrate and explore his faith in the visionary, lay in discovering the narrative means that would make his hero's ultimate metamorphosis convincing. He had a number of sources to draw upon, but which incidents to use, and how to arrange them, were matters he would have to work out for himself.[1]

So much has been written about *Endymion* in the last fifty years that the critic approaches it with some of the "lowliness of heart" Keats said he felt in starting its fourth book.[2] W. J. Bate has cautioned critics against any more "doomed ingenuity and the irritabilities of superfluous debate,"[3] and I hope that none will emerge in the following pages. But what strikes me as the best recent criticism of the poem is more or less agreed on two points: that *Endymion* is very much an apprentice work, and that Keats's faith in the validity of Endymion's visionary quest wavered during the eight months he spent writing the poem.[4] I want to argue that, by examining the numerous—perhaps too numerous—metamorphoses that occur throughout *Endymion* and give some shape to the overall narrative diffuseness, we can discern Keats's weakening trust of visionary experience.

It was, of course, Keats himself who first stressed that *Endymion* was primarily an apprentice work. From the start he viewed its composition as a way of honing his craftsmanship: "it will be a test, a trial of my Powers of Imagination and chiefly of my invention which is a rare thing indeed—by which I must make 4000 lines of one bare circumstances and fill them with Poetry" (I, 169-70).[5] Later Keats came to feel that he had failed the test miserably. In the poem's original, rejected preface he points out with foolhardy yet touching candor that "as I proceeded my steps were all uncertain," and the published preface forewarns the reader to "perceive great inexperience, immaturity, and every error denoting a feverish attempt, rather than a deed accomplished." [6] Each of the four books lacks "completion"; but no amount of verbal polishing would make the poem truly presentable, for "the foundations are too sandy" (a remark which suggests Keats's dissatisfaction with the myth's visionary premise).[7] "It is just that this youngster should die away." [8] Yet Keats continued to stress the poem's importance to him as a self-educating exercise. "My ideas with respect to it I assure you are very low," he wrote Bailey after completing Book III, but ". . . Rome was not built in a Day, and all the good I expect from my employment this summer is the fruit of Experience which I hope to gather in my next Poem" (I, 168). Similarly, in a letter written one year later to his publisher, Hessey, Keats labeled the poem "slip-shod":

That it is so is no fault of mine.—No!—though it may sound a little paradoxical. It is as good as I had power to make it—by myself—Had I been nervous about its being a perfect piece, & with that view asked advice, & trembled over every page, it would not have been written; for it is not in my nature to fumble—I will write independently.—I have written independently *without Judgment*—I may write independently *& with judgment hereafter.*—The genius of Poetry must work out its own salvation in a man: It cannot be matured by law & precept, but by sensation & watchfulness in itself—That which is creative must create itself—In Endymion, I leaped headlong into the Sea, and thereby have become better acquainted with the Soundings, the quicksands, & the rocks, than if I had stayed upon the green shore, and piped a silly pipe, and took tea & comfortable advice.

(I, 374)

On the basis of these remarks, it is sheer folly to expect a consistently worked-out allegorical scheme in *Endymion;* on the contrary, we are encouraged to find what in fact Shelley found: "treasures poured forth with indistinct profusion" (II, 311). The profusion was frankly intentional: "Do not the Lovers of Poetry like to have a little Region to wander in where they may pick and choose, and in which the images are so numerous that many are forgotten and found new in a second Reading: which may be food for a Week's stroll in the Summer?" (I, 170); but the indistinctness resulted from a conflict in Keats's attitude toward the visionary, which intensified as he continued to work on the poem.

One way of measuring the conflict is to contrast *Endymion*'s central argument, the well-known "fellowship with essence" speech in Book I, with the poem's concluding events: the Indian Maid's metamorphosis into Cynthia the moon-goddess and the earthly shepherd's transformative "enskying" (such as it is) among the immortals. We expect the ending to illustrate Endymion's argument; that it does so only in a partial and confused way betrays the work's intellectual discontinuity and Keats's skepticism at what the shepherd's transformation must inevitably mean.

In Book I, Endymion justifies his dream-intoxication to his troubled sister Peona by asking,

> "Wherein lies happiness? In that which becks
> Our ready minds to fellowship divine,
> A fellowship with essence; till we shine,
> Full alchemiz'd, and free of space."
>
> (I, 777-80)

These much-disputed opening lines of Endymion's long speech, which Keats regarded as crucial to his creative development (see *Letters*, I, 218), were added two months after he finished Book IV, and this has encouraged readers to view them as defining the poem's philosophical bias in favor of visionary yearning. The addition resembles some less exsspressive lines in Keats's fair copy, which were later canceled: for "fellowship divine" the fair copy has the more erotically tinged "blending pleasurable," followed by: "And that delight is the most treasurable / That makes the richest Alchymy." [9] But whether one interprets "essence" transcendentally or, as is more likely, in a material sense as synonymous with "A thing of beauty" (note line 795: " 'Feel we these things?' ") is perhaps not so important.[10] What is important is Endymion's contention that happiness lies in a sympathetic union with nature (the

" 'rose leaf' " whose texture " 'soothe[s]' " the lips [I, 782, 783]), with music (synechdochic for the arts), and with fellow human beings, first in friendship, then most intensely in love, which is said to *renovate* our being: it " 'genders a novel sense, / At which we start and fret; till in the end, / Melting into its radiance, we blend, / Mingle, and so become a part of it,—' " (I, 808-11).

That is, happiness lifts us from ordinary consciousness to a new, exalted plane of awareness, an idealized state of bliss akin to the immortal. " 'Feel we these things?—that moment we have stept / Into a sort of oneness, and our state / Is like a floating spirit's' " (I, 795-97). This is precisely the condition Endymion has experienced in his brief encounters with his goddess in Book I and longs to achieve permanently. We are prepared for a conclusion in which Endymion steps into a sort of oneness with Cynthia, whereupon his state will be that of a "floating spirit's"; however, this does not occur. We need now to examine how the actual events of the final scene of Book IV differ from our expectation, for that difference expresses the poem's true, if unintended, meaning.

First, the Indian Maid is metamorphosed into the divine Cynthia. Her change does not follow the customary pattern, but this can be easily accounted for. It does not constitute a real transformation of being, since the Indian Maid is in fact Cynthia in disguise, the purpose of which appears to be that of further testing Endymion's response to a human sorrow not his own (though it is her beauty, not her grief, which really attracts him: "And so he groan'd, as one by beauty slain" [IV, 98]). Since her discontent is feigned, simply a moral challenge for the hero, there is no impulse for Keats to resort to his usual metamorphosis pattern in order to rescue her from it (as we shall see him doing with Endymion throughout much of the poem). Instead, she undergoes an effortless, mechanical transformation, speaking "in a new voice, but sweet as love, / To Endymion's amaze" (recalling the wonderment of the lovers in "I stood tip-toe"):

And as she spake, into her face there came
Light, as reflected from a silver flame:
Her long black hair swell'd ampler, in display
Full golden; in her eyes a brighter day

Dawn'd blue and full of love. Aye, he beheld
Phoebe, his passion!

(IV, 978-79, 982-87)

Once her identity has been resolved, Cynthia prepares us for a
similarly miraculous change in Endymion: " 'from this mortal
state / Thou shouldst, my love, by some unlook'd for change / Be
spiritualiz'd' " (IV, 991-93). This is the point to which the entire
poem has been leading; and indeed, as if to heighten the bliss of
Endymion's imminent immortalization, Keats stresses, just prior to
the Indian Maid's change, his hero's massive discontent. Still un-
satisfied despite repeated promises of happiness, Endymion for-
swears his quest for ideal love as invalid (though his passion has
not dimmed):

"There never liv'd a mortal man, who bent
His appetite beyond his natural sphere,
But starv'd and died. My sweetest Indian, here,
Here will I kneel, for thou redeemed hast
My life from too thin breathing: gone and past
Are cloudy phantasms. Caverns lone, farewel!
And air of visions, and the monstrous swell
Of visionary seas!"

(IV, 646-53)

But Endymion's earthly redeemer then renounces him, declaring
her love to be "forbidden" (IV, 752), whereupon he plunges into
an explicitly morbid distress. He vows to Peona and the Maid that
he will become a hermit, and the three bewildered figures, "Striving their ghastly malady to cheer," wander to "a cypress grove . . .
[of] deadly maw" (IV, 897, 906). After requesting one last visit
with his mortal love before retreating to his hermit's cave, Endymion rests "His head upon a mossy hillock green, / And so
remain'd as he a corpse had been / All the long day . . ." (IV,
918-20). The time is now sunset, as in "I stood tip-toe" just before
the miraculous curing, and Endymion laments:

"Night will strew
On the damp grass myriads of lingering leaves,

And with them shall I die; nor much it grieves
To die, when summer dies on the cold sward. . . ."
"My kingdom's at its death, and just it is
That I should die with it:"
(IV, 933-36; 940-41)

"In sort of deathful glee," he muses "On things for which no word-
ing can be found; / Deeper and deeper sinking, until drown'd /
Beyond the reach of music" (IV, 945; 962-64). At this point, the
Indian Maid's metamorphosis occurs, and she announces Endymion's. But instead of portraying Endymion's transformation from
a state of morbid discontent to one of immortal bliss, Keats gives
us this:

Next Cynthia bright
Peona kiss'd, and bless'd with fair good night:
Her brother kiss'd her too, and knelt adown
Before his goddess, in a blissful swoon.
She gave her fair hands to him, and behold,
Before three swiftest kisses he had told,
They vanish'd far away!—Peona went
Home through the gloomy wood in wonderment.
(IV, 996-1003)

The metamorphosis pattern is discernible, but only in an impoverished form. Morbid discontent is followed by "a blissful
swoon," but then, instead of what the poem surely calls for,
namely, a triumphant celebration—at long last!—of Endymion's
enskying, his rise to a newly spiritualized state, he simply disap-
pears. Not only is there no celebration; there is no enskying. Or,
rather, it is implied but not dramatized.

Endymion's truncated metamorphosis signifies Keats's skepticism of the supramundane fate that he seems originally to have
intended for hero. The Greek myth, which since the winter of 1816
he had viewed as an apt vehicle for expressing his faith in visionary
experience, turned out to be something of an embarrassment. The
ending of *Endymion* is Keats's failed attempt to strike a compromise
between his visionary longing and a growing awareness of human
limitation, which raised moral questions incompatible with the

"endless bliss, / An immortality of passion" that Cynthia had promised to the shepherd (II, 807-8). The goddess's metamorphosis can succeed precisely because she is a goddess; the mortal's is an unconvincing aesthetic necessity. *Endymion* is, as John Middleton Murry has said, "a transition piece." [11] That is, it reveals Keats's struggle with the truthful impingement of the "agonies, the strife / Of human hearts" (dramatized in *Endymion* by the hero's extended love-sickness and his acquaintance with the suffering of others) upon his faith in the two poetic realms celebrated in "Sleep and Poetry"—those of Flora and of the visionary charioteer.

There are various indications throughout the narrative of Keats's skepticism, though none is quite so telling as Endymion's impoverished metamorphosis at the close. For example, just after the Indian Maid has told Endymion that she may not be his love, Keats apologizes to his desperate hero (and to his weary reader):

> Endymion! unhappy! it nigh grieves
> Me to behold thee thus in last extreme:
> Ensky'd ere this, but truly that I deem
> Truth the best music in a first-born song.
> Thy lute-voic'd brother will I sing ere long,
> And thou shalt aid—hast thou not aided me?
> Yes, moonlight Emperor! felicity
> Has been thy meed for many thousand years;
> Yet often have I, on the brink of tears,
> Mourn'd as if yet thou wert a forester,—
> Forgetting the old tale.
>
> (IV, 770-79)

The candor of this is disarming. Reminding us that *Endymion* is an apprentice work preparing him for a better poem about Apollo *(Hyperion)*, Keats admits that the truth of his current perceptions must take precedence over the formal demands of the "old tale." The truth is that Endymion's all-too-human suffering has become more vital to Keats than any immortal existence he might imagine for him.[12] Hence, at the conclusion, the old tale *is* half-forgotten, and Keats dwells more on Endymion's fate as a forester than as an immortal (Cynthia tells Peona, " 'we shall range / These forests . . .' " [IV, 993-94]).

The visionary world is, of course, challenged directly by Endymion himself in Book IV, when his adventures seem to have brought him nothing but disappointment: [13]

> "I have clung
> To nothing, lov'd a nothing, nothing seen
> Or felt but a great dream! O I have been
> Presumptuous against love, against the sky,
> Against all elements, against the tie
> Of mortals each to each. . . ."
>   (IV, 636-41) [14]

He longs for " 'one human kiss! / One sigh of real breath' " and " 'no more of dreaming' "—though he is not fully prepared to reject it: " 'Adieu, my daintiest Dream! although so vast / My love is still for thee' " (IV, 664-65, 669, 656-57).

Keats's struggle with the claims of the ideal and the real is most intense and intractable, as I have argued, at *Endymion's* conclusion, but it can be observed as well in the numerous episodes of metamorphosis in the poem's first three books. Here we must distinguish between two categories of metamorphosis (which, however, exist side by side): those experienced by the poem's secondary characters, and those undergone by Endymion himself. The difference in kind between these two categories corresponds to what we noted in the poem's final scene: the transformations of the minor figures, like Cynthia's, are complete, whereas those of Endymion, like his putative enskying, are always partial and inconclusive. But what is particularly striking about *all* these episodes is their common structure: repeatedly we can discern, with minor variations, the metamorphosis pattern of spiritual discontent, followed by a lapse of ordinary consciousness and the emergence of new life or awareness.

For example, Endymion's underworld wandering in Book II eventually takes him to the bower of Adonis, "Full of light, incense, tender minstrelsy, / And more of beautiful and strange beside" (II, 390-91). A Cupid attending the "sleeping youth" welcomes Endymion, " 'For 'tis the nicest touch of human honour, / When some ethereal and high-favouring donor / Presents immortal bowers to mortal sense' " (II, 393, 436-38). He is offered enchanted food and drink while the Cupid recounts Adonis' story; the nourishment is clearly symbolic of the vitalizing effect Adonis' reawakening is to have on Endymion.

Adonis' mortal discontent, of course, was the wound inflicted by the boar's tusk, ordered by Venus when Adonis spurned her love. But the repentant goddess then persuaded Jove to decree that Adonis " 'should be rear'd / Each summer time to life' " (II, 477-78). Hence the youth's death was averted; instead, he endures a six-month winter sleep when he is deprived of the warmth of actual love:

> "Aye, sleep; for when our love-sick queen did weep
> Over his waned corse, the tremulous shower
> Heal'd up the wound, and, with a balmy power,
> Medicined death to a lengthened drowsiness:"
> (II, 481-84)

Thus the mortally wounded Adonis, having lapsed into a magically preserving sleep, is now to be metamorphosed into a "new life" (II, 528). His revival is heralded by two events. First the other attendant Cupids are roused by mysterious voices that command " 'Once more sweet life begin!' " (II, 506). When "all were soon alive," "an air / Odorous and enlivening" descends from the arbour roof, reminiscent of the ethereal and pure breezes that penetrated the half-closed lattices of the sickroom in "I stood tip-toe" (II, 510, 513-14). Then Venus herself descends:

> Her shadow fell upon his breast, and charm'd
> A tumult to his heart, and a new life
> Into his eyes. Ah, miserable strife,
> But for her comforting! unhappy sight,
> But meeting her blue orbs! Who, who can write
> Of these first minutes? The unchariest muse
> To embracements warm as theirs makes coy excuse.
> (II, 527-33)

This stressful metamorphosis prefigures Apollo's dying into life in Book III of *Hyperion*—but with an important difference. Whereas the "fierce convulse" of Apollo's transformation is vividly detailed, Adonis' pain of rebirth is merely asserted; the poetry does not make us feel it. Still, Adonis' miserable yet blissful strife has dramatic relevance, for it corresponds to the nearly simultaneous joy and pain attendant upon Endymion's temporarily revitalizing encounters with his own goddess. Venus points the parallel between the lovers' plights when she invokes Cupid's aid on Endymion's behalf, saying, " 'That when through heavy hours I used to rue / The endless sleep of this new-born Adon', / This stranger ay I pitied' " (II, 553-55). Indicating the narrative purpose of the entire episode, she intimates Endymion's eventual transformation: " 'one day thou wilt be blest' " (II, 573), whereupon the immortal figures suddenly soar into the empyrean, obviously prefigurative of Endymion's own enskying: "At these words up flew / The impatient doves, up rose the floating car, / Up went the hum celestial. High afar / The Latmian saw them minish into nought" (II, 579-82). Endymion is properly encouraged:

> He did not rave, he did not stare aghast,
> For all those visions were o'ergone, and past,
> And he in loneliness: he felt assur'd
> Of happy times when all he had endur'd
> Would seem a feather to the mighty prize.
>   (II, 588-92)

But Endymion's reaction to the passing of these "visions" is one of calm reassurance only because he is a witness to them, not a participant; when his own vitalizing encounters with Cynthia dissolve, he does indeed "rave."

Whereas Venus' awakening of Adonis to new life is one of many discrete episodes in Book II, the single tale of Glaucus' enfeeblement and rejuvenation occupies nearly all of Book III. The theme of the book is the vitalizing power of love, which is announced in the Induction, a hymn to ethereal "regalities" whose majesty far outshines that of earthly rulers. The "gentlier-mightest" of these regalities—the Moon—"dost bless every where, with silver lip / Kissing dead things to life" (III, 43, 56-57). Endymion, as Cynthia's chosen lover, unwittingly becomes the agent of her saving power when he revitalizes the moribund Glaucus and the drowned lovers he has collected in a kind of undersea morgue.

When Endymion first encounters Glaucus, he effects a sudden change in the old man's body and spirit, which prefigures his more complete rejuvenation later on. Though Glaucus appears to sit "calm and peacefully" "in the concave green of the sea" (III, 192, 191), he suffers a withering death-in-life:

> And his white hair was awful, and a mat
> Of weeds were cold beneath his cold thin feet;
> And, ample as the largest winding-sheet,
> A cloak of blue wrapp'd up his aged bones. . . .
>
>   The old man rais'd his hoary head and saw
> The wilder'd stranger—seeming not to see,
> His features were so lifeless. Suddenly
> He woke as from a trance.
> (III, 194-97, 218-21)

As Glaucus will subsequently explain, it was Circe who a thousand years ago had so entranced him; now the mere sight of Endymion breaks the spell: " 'I saw thee, and my blood no longer cold / Gave mighty pulses: in this tottering case / Grew a new heart, which at this moment plays / As dancingly as thine' " (III, 304-7). In other words, Glaucus' glimpse of Endymion constitutes the lapse of what has become his customary consciousness, resulting in "a new heart." This is followed by the usual upward movement, here expressed in part by a striking simile, and Glaucus' joyous declaration of his imminent return to youth:

>   - his snow-white brows
> Went arching up, and like two magic ploughs
> Furrow'd deep wrinkles in his forehead large,
> Which kept as fixedly as rocky marge,
> Till round his wither'd lips had gone a smile.
> Then up he rose, like one whose tedious toil
> Had watch'd for years in forlorn hermitage,
> Who had not from mid-life to utmost age

Eas'd in one accent his o'er-burden'd soul
Even to the trees.

"O Jove! I shall be young again, be young!
O shell-borne Neptune, I am pierc'd and stung
With new-born life! What shall I do? Where go,
When I have cast this serpent-skin of woe?"—
"For I no more shall wither, droop, and pine.
Thou art the man!"
(III, 221-30, 237-40, 254-55)

Endymion, it turns out, is the saving presence whose arrival was prophesied in a scroll that Glaucus seized from the dying hand of a shipwrecked sailor. The scroll promised deliverance from *"His loath'd existence through ten centuries"* and eventual death if he would steep himself in magic lore and collect *"all lovers tempest-tost, / And in the savage overwhelming lost"*—

Which done, and all these labours ripened,
A youth, by heavenly power lov'd and led,
Shall stand before him; whom he shall direct
How to consummate all. The youth elect
Must do the thing, or both will be destroy'd.—
(III, 691, 703-4, 707-11)

The narrative purpose of Endymion's encounter with Glaucus is by now clear: under the old man's tutelage, he is to witness love's transforming power. With brotherly affection Glaucus thanks Endymion for opening " 'The prison gates that have so long opprest / My weary watching' " and attributes Endymion's being " 'commission'd' " for the ensuing ritual to his ardent desire: " 'Aye, hadst thou never lov'd an unknown power, / I had been grieving at this joyous hour' " (III, 296, 298, 301-2).

As they speed toward their "joyous task," "this young soul in age's mask" tells Endymion the story of his life (III, 309, 310). His history divides into three phases each of which is structured by the metamorphosis pattern. A thousand years ago Glaucus led a lonely but protected and comfortable life as a fisherman, providing the poor folk of the sea-country with daily sustenance (paralleling the shepherd-prince's beneficence toward the Latmians prior to his dream visions). But he " 'began / To feel distemper'd longings: to desire / The utmost privilege that ocean's sire / Could grant in benediction: to be free / Of [i.e., within] all his kingdom. Long in misery / I wasted . . .' " (III, 374-79). The lapse of ordinary consciousness comes when Glaucus plunges into the sea, " 'To interknit / One's senses with so dense a breathing stuff' " (III, 381-82). His subsequent new existence as a sea creature is pure delight: " 'At first I dwelt / Whole days and days in sheer astonishment; / Forgetful utterly of self intent . . . / 'Twas freedom! and at once I visited / The ceaseless wonders of this ocean-bed' " (III, 384-86, 391-92).

This pleasurable existence is short-lived, however, for Glaucus falls in love with the immortal Scylla, whose customary rebuff engenders a new kind of distempered longing in her latest suitor. In his " 'too fierce agony to bear,' " Glaucus seeks relief from Circe (III, 410). He rears his head above the water and lapses into " 'a swoon' " that " 'Left me dead-drifting to that fatal power' " (III, 416, 417). He wakes up, at dawn, in a garden of earthly delights:

"How sweet, and sweeter! for I heard a lyre,
And over it a sighing voice expire.
It ceased—I caught light footsteps; and anon
The fairest face that morn e'er look'd upon
Push'd through a screen of roses. Starry Jove!
With tears, and smiles, and honey-words she wove
A net whose thraldom was more bliss than all
The range of flower'd Elysium."

(III, 421-28)

Unable to resist Circe's blandishments, he promptly forgets Scylla: " 'The current of my former life was stemm'd, / And to this arbitrary queen of sense / I bow'd a tranced vassal,' " luxuriating in " 'new born delights' " (III, 458-60, 472).

Yet Glaucus' new life of earthly pleasure is as transient as his underwater freedom had been. Concluding his tale, he tells Endymion " 'How specious heaven was changed to real hell' " (III, 476).[15] He awakes one morning ready " 'to slake / My greedy thirst' " with draughts of love, only to find Circe missing— " 'Whereat the barbed shafts / Of disappointment stuck in me so sore, / That out I ran and search'd the forest o'er' " (III, 478-79, 480-82). This disappointment initiates a long series of spiritual and physical discontents from which Glaucus is partially relieved by his glimpse of Endymion and is ultimately delivered by the ceremony of rejuvenation that they jointly perform. First, he sees " 'A sight too fearful for the feel of fear' "—Circe tyrannizing her deformed lovers (whom she bloats with air and metamorphoses into a huge Python, which vanishes); next, he hears Circe pronounce his sentence: " '. . . Live and wither, cripple and still breathe / Ten hundred years: which gone, I then bequeath / Thy fragile bones to unknown burial' " (III, 496, 597-99); then he finds Scylla dead by Circe's hand; and finally he becomes decrepit, but receives the scroll prophesying his possible salvation.

It is from this woeful, debilitated state that Glaucus is now to be metamorphosed with Endymion's help. They travel to "that crystal place" where "Poor lovers lay at rest from joys and woes" and begin a series of magic rituals to effect Glaucus' rejuvenation and the mass revitalizing of the drowned (III, 735, 736). These rituals are the equivalent of the sleeps and swoons that we encounter in similar Keatsian metamorphoses. In a priestly gesture, Endymion scatters torn bits of the scroll on his congregation, who instantly change and arise:

> Endymion from Glaucus stood apart,
> And scatter'd in his face some fragments light.
> How lightning-swift the change! a youthful wight
> Smiling beneath a coral diadem,
> Out-sparkling sudden like an upturn'd gem,
> Appeared, and, stepping to a beauteous corse,
> Kneel'd down beside it, and with tenderest force
> Press'd its cold hand, and wept,—and Scylla sigh'd!
> Endymion, with quick hand, the charm applied—
> The nymph arose: he left them to their joy,
> And onward went upon his high employ,

Showering those powerful fragments on the dead.
And, as he pass'd, each lifted up its head,
As doth a flower at Apollo's touch.
Death felt it to his inwards: 'twas too much:
Death fell a weeping in his charnel-house.
The Latmian persever'd along, and thus
All were re-animated

(III, 773-90)

The scene is strongly reminiscent of the end of "I stood tip-toe,"
both in its overall joyous mood and in specific narrative details:
the lovers "sprang to each other madly" (cf. "I stood tip-toe," 227-
28), while "Delicious symphonies, like airy flowers, / Budded, and
swell'd, and, full-blown, shed full flowers / Of light, soft, unseen
leaves of sounds divine" (III, 798-800)—this music echoes the cured
lovers speaking "in poesy" at the close of the earlier poem.

The procession of revived lovers moves to Neptune's palace,
where Venus comforts Endymion, the sole figure whose condition
has not been altered by the magic rites: " 'What, not yet / Escap'd
from dull mortality's harsh net? / A little patience, youth! 'twill
not be long . . .' " (III, 906-8). But Venus is wrong, for Keats still
has a thousand lines to write. First, he must return his hero to the
earth, which he accomplishes by resorting once again to the metamorphosis pattern. Overwhelmed by the festivities in Neptune's
palace ("He could not bear it—shut his eyes in vain" [III, 1008]),
Endymion shouts, " 'Oh, I shall die!' " and "At Neptune's feet he
sank. A sudden ring / Of Nereids were about him, in kind strife /
To usher back his spirit into life: / But still he slept" (III, 1010,
1013-16). As the Nereids transport him, Endymion hears a voice:
"Immortal bliss for me too thou hast won. / Arise then!" whereupon "The
youth at once arose" (III, 1024-25, 1028). Now back on earth, Endymion is about to meet the Indian Maid and enter upon another
long spell of spiritual strife.

As the ending of Book III indicates, Keats often uses the metamorphosis pattern simply to propel his narrative forward. This is
especially true in the poem's first two books, where Endymion's
discontent is repeatedly—but only provisionally—resolved by a
swoon leading to reanimation, which is followed in turn by a new

wave of discontent. But more than narrative strategy is involved here, especially when one considers the inconclusiveness of these metamorphoses in the light of what happens to Endymion in the final scene. In contrast to figures like Adonis and Glaucus, he is never permitted to achieve a *full* transformation of being. As Sperry rightly notes, "The major action of the poem does not follow the pattern of gradual ascent but resembles more the parabolic structure we have seen emerge for the first time in the central vision of 'Sleep and Poetry,' a pattern of longing, momentary fulfillment, then loss, despondency, and doubt." [16] What is being doubted is nothing less than the validity of the entire visionary question.

But while Endymion's provisional, incomplete metamorphoses do hint at a covert distrust of the visionary, their primary purpose, especially early in the poem, is merely to advance the narrative. For example, the metamorphosis pattern is discernible in the poem's first significant dramatic action: Endymion's confrontation with his sister Peona. [17] Prior to it the shepherd-prince has been introduced as a heroic youth blighted by some mysterious malady:

> A smile was on his countenance; he seem'd,
> To common lookers on, like one who dream'd
> Of idleness in groves Elysian:
> But there were some who feelingly could scan
> A lurking trouble in his nether lip,
> And see that oftentimes the reins would slip
> Through his forgotten hands. . . .
> (I, 175-81)

Among the elders of Latmos, "vieing to rehearse / Each one his own anticipated bliss" in Elysium, Endymion stands distracted: "His senses had swoon'd off"; ". . . in the self-same fix'd trance he kept, / Like one who on the earth had never stept— / Aye, even as dead-still as a marble man . . ." (I, 372-73, 398, 403-5). Peona, "like some midnight spirit nurse / Of happy changes in emphatic dreams," then leads Endymion to an arbor on a bowery island, where "Soon was he quieted to slumbrous rest" (I, 413-14, 442). Keats's subsequent apostrophe to sleep's revitalizing power indi-

cates how we are to regard all the analogous lapses of ordinary
consciousness that occur throughout the poem (and beyond it):

> O magic sleep! O comfortable bird,
> That broodest o'er the troubled sea of the mind
> Till it is hush'd and smooth! O unconfin'd
> Restraint! imprisoned liberty! great key
> To golden palaces, strange minstrelsy,
> Fountains grotesque, new trees, bespangled caves,
> Echoing grottos, full of tumbling waves
> And moonlight; aye, to all the mazy world
> Of silvery enchantment!—who, upfurl'd
> Beneath thy drowsy wing a triple hour,
> But renovates and lives?—Thus, in the bower,
> Endymion was calm'd to life again.
> Opening his eyelids with a healthier brain,
> He said: "I feel this thine endearing love
> All through my bosom. . . ."
>
> (I, 453-67)

But Peona realizes her brother has been merely consoled, not
cured, by his rest, and she importunes him to explain the cause of
his secret malady. Endymion then describes his wandering to a
favored nook where, just as the sun disappeared below the horizon,
" 'There blossom'd suddenly a magic bed / Of sacred ditamy, and
poppies red: / At which I wondered greatly . . .' " (I, 554-56).
" 'Dizzy and distraught' " at this mysterious transformation of the
landscape, Endymion is lulled to sleep by a breeze blowing
through the poppies (I, 565ff.). There follows his first dream-vision
of Cynthia, an unmistakable sexual fantasy of soaring in space and
loitering amidst honeyed flowers (I, 650-71). Endymion fears that
the overpowering eroticism of their union will kill him; instead, it
vitalizes his spirit to experience pleasures unfelt before:

> "I was distracted; madly did I kiss
> The wooing arms which held me, and did give
> My eyes at once to death: but 'twas to live,

To take in draughts of life from the gold fount
Of kind and passionate looks; to count, and count
The moments, by some greedy help that seem'd
A second self, that each might be redeem'd
And plunder'd of its load of blessedness.
Ah, desperate mortal! I ev'n dar'd to press
Her very cheek against my crowned lip,
And, at that moment, felt my body dip
Into a warmer air: a moment more,
Our feet were soft in flowers. There was store
Of newest joys upon that alp."

(I, 653-66)

Of course, these newest joys must fade: " 'my sweet dream / Fell into nothing—into stupid sleep' " (I, 677-78). Endymion awakes disconsolate, and nature, reflecting his mood, appears sickly:

". . . all the pleasant hues
Of heaven and earth had faded: deepest shades
Were deepest dungeons; heaths and sunny glades
Were full of pestilent light; our taintless rills
Seem'd sooty, and o'er-spread with upturn'd gills
Of dying fish; the vermeil rose had blown
In frightful scarlet, and its thorns out-grown
Like spiked aloe."

(I, 691-98)

Cynthia visits Endymion twice more (when he is awake), and these episodes, while less extensive than the first, have many details in common with it. What Endymion says of his third meeting with his unknown lover is true for all of them: each time he has been " 'tortured with renewed life' " (I, 919).

The torturous cycle persists in Book II. Endymion is wandering in an underground realm devoid of vegetation—"One faint eternal eventide of gems" and marble rooms (II, 225). The absence of life around him causes Endymion to turn inward; but "how crude and sore / The journey homeward to habitual self!" (II, 275-76). He is afflicted with "The deadly feel of solitude: for lo! / He cannot see the heavens, nor the flow / Of rivers, nor hill-flowers running wild . . ." (II, 284-86). "Surcharg'd with grief," he prays to Diana in her role as huntress for relief, which she grants by magically transforming the marble waste into a lush garden (obviously a repeat of her metamorphosing the landscape prior to first visiting Endymion):

> . . . sweeter than the rill
> To its old channel, or a swollen tide
> To margin sallows, were the leaves he spied,
> And flowers, and wreaths, and ready myrtle crowns
> Up heaping through the slab: refreshment drowns
> Itself, and strives its own delights to hide—
> Nor in one spot alone; the floral pride
> In a long whispering birth enchanted grew
> Before his footsteps. . . .
>
> (II, 339-47)

This birth of flowers begets a sudden change in Endymion's state of mind: "Increasing still in heart, and pleasant sense, / Upon his fairy journey on he hastes" (II, 351-52). Yet Endymion's buoyant spirits droop almost immediately thereafter, for he is still alone, and the music he now hears makes him more melancholy than ever.

Endymion's prolonged discontent is resolved, as we have seen, only by an unconvincing narrative contrivance at the end of Book IV, when Keats had surely tired of writing the poem and was eager to begin a new work. There is, however, much to be said for John Middleton Murry's argument that the poem's "psychological culmination" occurs prior to the narrative close—that *Endymion's* actual resolution of the human issues it raises is the "Cave of Quietude" passage, not the Indian Maid's metamorphosis into Cynthia and Endymion's putative enskying.[18]

The Cave of Quietude is Keats's symbolic name for the mind's capacity to pass beyond despair so that life may be continued. It represents a kind of spiritual courage in the form of grace, for it cannot be willed: "Enter none / Who strive therefore: on the sudden it is won. / Just when the sufferer begins to burn, / Then it is free to him; and from an urn, / Still fed by melting ice, he takes a draught—" (IV, 531-35). This symbolic drinking (analogous to the swoons and sleeps of similar metamorphic passages) signifies the soul's transition from a potentially fatal torment to a state in which "the whole being of the sufferer is bathed and renewed": [19]

> There lies a den,
> Beyond the seeming confines of the space
> Made for the soul to wander in and trace
> Its own existence, of remotest glooms.
> Dark regions are around it, where the tombs
> Of buried griefs the spirit sees, but scarce
> One hour doth linger weeping, for the pierce
> Of new-born woe it feels more inly smart:
> And in these regions many a venom'd dart
> At random flies; they are the proper home
> Of every ill: the man is yet to come
> Who hath not journeyed in this native hell.
> But few have ever felt how calm and well
> Sleep may be had in that deep den of all.
> There anguish does not sting; nor pleasure pall:
> Woe-hurricanes beat ever at the gate,
> Yet all is still within and desolate.
> Beset with plainful gusts, within ye hear
> No sound so loud as when on curtain'd bier
> The death-watch tick is stifled.
>   (IV, 512-31)

The mysterious transformation of suffering into a contemplative acceptance of what suffering means must be expressed paradoxically, for the experience implies a loss of hope as well as a gain in wisdom:

> Happy gloom!
> Dark paradise! Where pale becomes the bloom
> Of health by due; where silence dreariest
> Is most articulate; where hopes infest;

Where those eyes are the brightest far that keep
Their lids shut longest in a dreamless sleep.
O happy spirit-home! O wondrous soul!
Pregnant with such a den to save the whole
In thine own depth. Hail, gentle Carian!
For, never since thy griefs and woes began,
Hast thou felt so content: a grievous feud
Hath led thee to this Cave of Quietude.
                              (IV, 537-48)

The soul's renewed state is not, so to speak, pure, as is Adonis'
when he is reunited with Venus after his stressful awakening, as is
Glaucus' when he regains his youth after a millennium of suffering,
as is, presumably, Endymion and Cynthia's when they achieve
"Immortal bliss" (III, 1024) after their various trials. Rather, it is a
matured awareness of the dialectic of desire and the limits of desire. Keats recognizes that both are native to the human soul; he is
neither a puritan nor a cynic. He is the uninhibited natural man
coming to terms with natural inhibitions.

When Endymion told Peona in Book I that happiness lies in a
fellowship with essence whose highest expression is human love, he
undoubtedly voiced one of Keats's most cherished convictions; but
as the poet's experience broadened, his perception of the essences
measured by the "Pleasure Thermometer"—nature, art, human re-
lations—became increasingly complex. Fellowship cannot be won
simply by desire, since the essences themselves are alive and can
act in ways that are often surprising (one thinks immediately of the
Grecian urn). The Cave of Quietude is in effect a recognition of
this, and as such constitutes Keats's more deeply felt response to
Endymion's original question. Happiness, that is, lies partly in the
realization that it is indeed a mixed blessing, for it entails a knowledge of its own mutability. The Cave of Quietude signals Keats's
entrance into what he will later call the "chamber of Maiden-
Thought," whose exploration led him to his finest poetry.

Why, then, did Keats revise the "Wherein lies happiness?" passage two months after completing *Endymion?* Does not "fellowship
divine, / A fellowship with essence" fail to deal with aspects of the
soul's journeying that the humane wisdom of the Cave of Quietude

can and does encompass? Herein lies the divided nature of the poem. Bate convincingly explains the revision as a last-minute attempt at unity: "The new lines suggested more of a bridge than had existed before between Endymion's hedonistic thought, as expressed in the original speech to Peona, and the idea he was seeking: they did so by putting that speech as an aspiration of the heart (however impossible of *complete* fulfillment)." [20] They express "a hope the poem had not genuinely fulfilled," but which, we must add, Keats could never entirely abandon, given his understanding of the poetic process and his persistent yearning for a new life of the soul.[21] Yet, after *Endymion,* the locus of the soul's habitation was more open to question than ever. During the remainder of his creative years, Keats was to explore various dark passages in life's Mansion; some of them, such as the *Hyperion* poems, would turn out to be culs-de-sac.

Notes

1. For a complete summary of Keats's sources, see *Keats: The Complete Poems,* ed. Miriam Allott (London: Longman, 1970), pp. 116-17.
2. The two main critical approaches to *Endymion*—the Neoplatonic and the erotic—are summarized by Sperry, *Keats the Poet,* pp. 91-93. Bate's description of the poem as an "allegory manqué" is apt: "the allegorical intention remains, though it becomes thinned, distracted, and ultimately divided" (*John Keats,* p. 174). Sperry concurs: "It is, in fact, allegory in its broadest and most general sense that characterizes *Endymion.* There is no reason for believing Keats began his poem with a plan for its development or its ultimate significance clearly in view. Quite the opposite is, in all likelihood, the case. Yet, at the same time, there is every reason to believe that he looked upon the composition as a necessary 'test, a trial,' as he himself put it, not merely of his 'Powers of Imagination' (I, 169) but of his deepest instincts and beliefs. The poem must crystallize, if only for himself, the most important of his poetic convictions. Above all it must confront the whole question of visionary experience that had emerged throughout the early verse, concentrated in his fascination with the legend of Endymion" (*Keats the Poet,* p. 95).
3. Bate, *John Keats,* p. 169.
4. The best explication of the poem's divided nature is the essay by Glen O. Allen, "The Fall of Endymion: A Study in Keats's Intellectual Growth," *Keats-Shelley Journal* 6 (1957): 37-57.

5. The "one bare circumstance" is usually taken to mean Endymion's infatuation with Cynthia, but it may refer—as I think it does—to his ultimate immortalization.

6. *Keats: The Complete Poems,* ed. M. Allott, pp. 775, 119.

7. Ibid., p. 119.

8. Ibid.

9. *The Poems of John Keats,* ed. Stillinger, p. 125.

10. The publishers were ready to print Endymion's question about happiness, following it directly with the image of the rose leaf, when Keats asked Taylor to insert the newly written lines after the question. He explained the change in a letter that has often been somewhat misinterpreted: "You must indulge me by putting this in for setting aside the badness of the other, such a preface is necessary to the Subject. The whole thing must I think have appeared to you, who are a consequitive Man, as a thing almost of mere words—but I assure you that when I wrote it, it was a regular stepping of the Imagination
                                                            Argument
    toward A Truth. My having written that <passage> will perhaps be of the greatest Service to me of anything I ever did—It set before me at once the gradations of Happiness even like a kind of Pleasure Thermometer—" (I, 218).

    In acknowledging the importance of "that Argument" (he first wrote "passage"), Keats is not referring merely, as is often assumed, to the newly added lines 777-80 (which he calls a "preface . . . necessary to the Subject" of happiness) but, rather, to the entire passage. Clearly he assumes Taylor's prior acquaintance with "the whole thing"; moreover, it is the lines that *follow* the famous phrase "a fellowship with essence" that describe the "gradations of Happiness" that Keats found so serviceable. If we read the letter in this way, we shall not dwell irritably on the presumably crucial thematic implications in the change from the erotic "blending pleasurable" to the possibly transcendental "fellowship divine, / A fellowship with essence" but, rather, focus our attention where Keats did, on "the whole thing." The new lines are a necessary clarification of those in the fair copy, not a significant alteration of them.

11. John Middleton Murry, *Keats* (New York: Noonday Press, 1955), p. 179.

12. See Murry's discussion of "Truth the best music of a first-born song," in *Keats,* pp. 166-79.

13. Peona also challenges visionary experience at I, 710-60, where she argues for a life of worldly achievement and urges Endymion to reject visions and dreams—"thoughts so sick" (I, 758).

14. Sperry's comment on these and similar lines is worth stressing: "For critics of the older school such speeches are only the final darkness before the onrushing dawn, Endymion's last moment of doubt before the revelation that the conflicting attractions that confront him are in fact but different aspects of a single ideal. Such a reading, whatever its validity as an ex post facto judgment, betrays the deeper meaning of the poem considered as a process of

creative self-discovery. For it ignores the tone of real conviction and dramatic urgency that characterizes the struggle in Book Four and, by contrast, the brief and remarkably spiritless conclusion" *(Keats the Poet,* pp. 110-11).

15. Sperry rightly sees the Circe episode as a challenge to the validity of visionary experience: "The rose-canopied bower where Circe promises him the supreme enjoyment of 'a long love dream' (iii.440) seems to reflect ironically on both the Bower of Adonis and certain aspects of the love-making between Endymion and Cynthia. . . . His infatuation and its end in powerlessness and withered age represent a caricature of the whole notion of the romantic quest which inevitably raises certain questions concerning Endymion's own pursuit" *(Keats the Poet,* pp. 107-8).

16. Ibid., pp. 100-101.

17. This scene is immediately preceded by the Latmians' "Hymn to Pan," the god of universal nature whose blessings are celebrated and reinvoked as the planting season begins: "be still the leaven, / That spreading in this dull and clodded earth / Gives it a touch ethereal—a new birth" (I, 296-98).

18. Murry, *Keats,* p. 176. "The self-exploration and experience of Keats in *Endymion* end in the Cave of Quietude—in the peace and unity which he suddenly found beyond and through the extremity of despair caused by the self-division which ensued on loyalty to contradictory passions of the Heart" (p. 176).

19. Ibid., p. 175.

20. Bate, *John Keats,* p. 184 (italics added).

21. Ibid., p. 184.

3.

Hyperion: The Sorrow of the Time

Hyperion should have been Keats's masterpiece; instead, it is a brilliant failure. The brilliance, of course, is in large part stylistic; as has often been noted, *Hyperion* approaches the sublimity of Miltonic blank verse more closely than any other English poem of Keats's day or of ours. But the poem is also notably ambitious in its thematic range: the myth of the fall of the Titans and their usurpation by the new generation of gods is made to symbolize a universal dilemma in the transfer of power, thereby encompassing contemporary political trends whose motive force is the Enlightenment belief in progress, as well as Keats's own personal quest for poetic maturity and ideal poetic beauty.[1] The difficulty is that the poem was not able to satisfy these simultaneous symbolic demands equally; indeed, it can be argued that Keats's recognition of this disequilibrium caused him to leave the poem in its fragmentary state. Still, as Sperry notes, "one can judge the poem's failure only in the light of the magnitude of the assimilation Keats hoped to achieve." [2]

The somber, dignified tone and sureness of versification in *Hyperion*'s first two books (and in much of the third) is in such striking contrast to Keats's previous work that one readily assents to Aileen Ward's remark that in September 1818 he had "become a different person from the man who had written *Endymion* a year ago." [3] It may be helpful, then, to review briefly Keats's activities during this longest interval between major works in the poet's short career, with an eye toward how they ultimately became incorporated in *Hyperion*.

In general, it was a time of very accelerated emotional and intellectual maturing. In a letter to Haydon of January 23, 1818, Keats contrasts the completed *Endymion* with his new poetic intentions:

> . . . the nature of *Hyperion* will lead me to treat it in a more naked and grecian Manner—and the march of passion and endeavour will be undeviating—and one great contrast between [the protagonists] will be—that the Hero of the written tale being mortal is led on, like Buonaparte, by circumstances; whereas the Apollo in *Hyperion* being a fore-seeing God will shape his actions like one.
>
> (I, 207)

Although this last desire was not actually fulfilled, it is worth noting that from the start Apollo—and not Hyperion—is the focus of Keats's interest. Moreover, his distinction between the two protagonists has a certain relevance to his own condition as poet. Keats had been led on in *Endymion* by "one bare circumstance," which he compelled himself to fill with four thousand lines of poetry. But there is the hope, at least, that Apollo, eventually introduced as the "Father of all verse" (III, 13), will be more forthright and self-controlled. This, in turn, would depend on a clear conception of Apollo's identity as the father of all verse; but that is precisely what Keats at present lacked (and, indeed, puzzled over throughout his career). As Murry contends, this is probably why Keats delayed so long before beginning the new poem.[4] Also inchoate at this time was Keats's understanding of "the agonies, the strife / Of human hearts"—he was as perplexed as his friend Bailey, who had exclaimed " *'Why should Woman suffer?'* " "These things are," Keats answered simply, "and he who feels how incompetent the most skyey Knight errantry is to heal this bruised fairness is like a sensitive leaf on the hot hand of thought" (I, 209). So much for Calidore and the other sworn protectors of womanhood in the 1817 *Poems*. Similarly, all his friends seemed just now involved in competitive wrangling, in which Keats wisely chose not to take sides: "It is unfortunate—Men should bear with each other—there lives not the Man who may not be cut up, aye hashed to pieces on his weakest side" (I, 210). Both concerns—the suffering of women and the quarreling of men—indicate Keats's steadily broadening awareness of social conflict; [5] and both make their way into *Hyperion* in the figures of Thea and Clymene and in the council of the defeated Titans in Book II. Similarly, Keats's urging of tolerance amid his friends' disputes will be heard again in Oceanus' exhortation to his fellow Titans: " 'Now comes the pain of truth, to whom 'tis pain; / O folly! for to bear all naked truths, / And to envisage circumstance, all calm, / That is the top of sovereignty' " (II, 202-5).

Still, Keats's apprehension of the conflict between will and destiny was too acute and insistent simply to be assuaged with the balm of tolerance. It had to be continually proved on the pulses, for only then would it be truly comprehended. This is the theme of Keats's fine sonnet, "On Sitting Down to Read *King Lear* Once Again."

> O golden-tongued Romance, with serene lute!
> >   Fair plumed syren, queen of far-away!
> >   Leave melodizing on this wintry day,
> Shut up thine olden pages, and be mute.   (4)
> Adieu! for, once again, the fierce dispute
> >   Betwixt damnation and impassion'd clay
> >   Must I burn through; once more humbly assay
> The bitter-sweet of this Shakespearean fruit.   (8)
> Chief Poet! and ye clouds of Albion,
> >   Begetters of our deep eternal theme!
> When through the old oak forest I am gone,
> >   Let me not wander in a barren dream: (12)
> But, when I am consumed in the fire,
> Give me new phoenix wings to fly at my desire.

Keats bids an extended farewell to a world, summed up in "Romance," to which he feels a deep attachment; this lingering valediction obliquely stresses the high importance he attributes to the alternate world of Tragedy, which he now wishes to embrace. That is, the contrast between aesthetic modes expresses a moral compulsiveness that is the true basis for the sonnet's tension and power. Keats's juxtaposition of images in the poem is expert. Whereas the imagery of the first quatrain is consistently aural and creates the requisite sense of distance through reiterated personifications, that of the second is immediate in its appeal to touch and taste, the primary Keatsian senses. Moreover, the images of fire and fruit in the second quatrain form a subtle linking of pagan and biblical ideas, which conveys the psychological need that underlies the poem. The fierce dispute between the inflamed human will ("impassion'd clay" signifies Lear as Adamic) and a subsuming fiery destiny must not merely be felt but transcended: "Must I burn *through.*" This transcendence is hinted at in the phrase "bittersweet . . . Shakespearean fruit" and clarified by the concluding phoenix image. Indeed, lines 7-8 can be seen as an inversion of Eve's experience in the Garden. For whereas Eve, not "humbly" but proudly, tasted of the fruit and subsequently fell from grace, the submissive Keats, having put aside innocent Romance to enter his own "old oak forest," hopes his tasting of the Shakespearean fruit will lead not to a fall but, rather, to a metaphorical ascent: "Give me new phoenix wings to fly at my desire." (This, too, points toward *Hyperion:* the poet is willing for himself the kind of transformative experience undergone by Apollo at the climax of the poem, and Saturn is an avatar of Lear.) Just as Romance is to be supplanted by Tragedy, so is the old Keats to be consumed in the fire of empathic suffering and thereby metamorphosed into a newly fledged poet who may then "fly at" his desire. Eve's was one kind of transformative experience, and though her fall led to worldly suffering, it also provided the possibility of ultimate salvation. Keats's anticipated experience takes this notion of *felix culpa* and renders it wholly conscious: he imaginatively embraces suffering ("our deep eternal theme") by rereading *King Lear* because he feels it will lead to his own desired salvation, which is nothing less than

the ability to write a new kind of poetry, requiring a deep awareness of humanity's "fierce dispute" with the limits of destiny. Evidently the thought of rereading the play precipitated some sort of
new awareness, for, as Keats told his brothers, "I think a little
change has taken place in my intellect lately," of which the sonnet
is then offered as illustration (I, 214).

Although the narrative element in the *Lear* sonnet is slight, it
does posit a chronological sequence, which permits us to discern all
the elements of the Keatsian metamorphosis pattern: an initial
state of discontent (here, Keats's compulsive need to reread *Lear*); a
deathlike lapse of normal consciousness (here, a kind of voluntary
vicarious immolation), leading to a new awareness, an enriched
sense of life's complexity, symbolized by a flight upward to a new
realm.

But the *Lear* sonnet, like Keats's earlier credo "Sleep and Poetry," is mainly prospective and therefore to some extent artificial;
quite different is the verse-letter "To John Hamilton Reynolds,
Esq." written two months later (March 25, 1818), a chilling record
of experience proved upon the pulses. Writing to his ailing friend,
Keats recoils from the tragic spectacle of natural law:

> . . . I saw
> Too far into the sea; where every maw
> The greater on the less feeds evermore:—
> But I saw too distinct into the core
> Of an eternal fierce destruction,
> And so from happiness I far was gone.
> Still am I sick of it:
>
> (93-99)

The verse-letter measures how much Keats's sense of human life
had darkened since "Sleep and Poetry," with its carefree celebration of Flora and old Pan, whose soothing power must now contend directly with nature's greater destructive force:

> and though to-day
> I've gathered young spring-leaves, and flowers gay
> Of periwinkle and wild strawberry,

Still do I that most fierce destruction see,
The shark at savage prey—the hawk at pounce,
The gentle robin, like a pard or ounce,
Ravening a worm.—Away ye horrid moods,
Moods of one's mind!

(99-106)

But the poem is also a regression from the desire to embrace the tragic vision expressed in the *Lear* sonnet. Such vacillation, of course, merely indicates how far Keats's imaginative intent was in advance of his actual experience. Yet *Hyperion* could not be begun until the two were more closely aligned.

The letters of this period hint at the psychological adjustments experience was demanding of Keats. In an unexpectedly grave revelation, he tells Taylor that happiness—Endymion's fervently pursued goal—he now considers to be an illusion:

> Young men for some time have an idea that such a thing as happiness is to be had and therefore are extremely impatient under any unpleasant restraining—in time however, of such stuff is the world about them, they know better and instead of striving from Uneasiness greet it as an habitual sensation, a pannier which is to weigh upon them through life.
>
> (I, 270)

Uneasiness was indeed becoming habitual, its principal causes at this time being George's imminent departure for America and Tom's unmistakable drift toward death. The prospect of loneliness inevitably stirred Keats's "horrid Morbidity of Temperament," though even as it burst forth it was characteristically assuaged by the vital consolation of art. Just prior to his Scotch tour, Keats wrote to Bailey:

> . . . I am never alone without rejoicing that there is such a thing as death—without placing my ultimate in the glory of dying for a great human purpose. Perhaps if my affairs were in a different state I could not have written the above—you shall judge—I have two Brothers one is driven by the "burden

of Society" to America the other, with an exquisite love of
Life, is in a lingering state— . . . I have a Sister too and may
not follow them, either to America or to the Grave—Life must
be undergone, and I certainly derive a consolation from the
thought of writing one or two more Poems before it ceases.

(I, 293)

Poetry would conquer even the fracturing of his parentless family,
just as in *Hyperion* the father of all verse would comprehend the
disintegration of that other ill-fated family, the Titans.

Simultaneous with Keats's coming to grips with these various
anxieties was a new thirsting for what he called "knowledge," by
which he meant not just erudition, but more importantly an understanding of the human mind, whose conflict with natural limitation as well as with its own contradictory impulses constituted,
in Wordsworth's memorable phrase, "the burthen of the mystery."
"I know nothing I have read nothing," Keats exclaimed to Taylor,
"and I mean to follow Solomon's directions of 'get Wisdom—get
understanding'—I find cavalier days are gone by. I find that I can
have no enjoyment in the World but continual drinking of Knowledge" (I, 271). The same notion is taken up and expanded in the
great letter to Reynolds of May 3, 1818, in which knowledge is
conceived in terms of its medicinal effect on the mind:

An extensive knowledge is needful to thinking people—it takes
away the heat and fever; and helps, by widening speculation,
to ease the Burden of the Mystery: a thing I begin to understand a little. . . . The difference of high Sensations with and
without knowledge appears to me this—in the latter case we
are falling continually ten thousand fathons deep and being
blown up again without wings and with all the horror of a
bare shouldered Creature—in the former case, our shoulders
are fledge, and we go thro' the same air and space without
fear. This is running one's rigs on the score of abstracted bene-
fit—when we come to human Life and the affections it is impossible [to know] how a parallel of breast and head can be
drawn—(you will forgive me for thus privately treading out
[of] my depth and take it for treading as schoolboys tread the

waters)—it is impossible to know how far knowledge will console us for the death of a friend and the ill "that flesh is heir to"—

(I, 277-78)

The skepticism that concludes this passage is characteristic and points toward another aspect of the drama of the Titans' fall in *Hyperion*, for even when their "high Sensations" of grief have been offered the ballast of Oceanus' tempering knowledge, the Titans remain miserable. Keats's distinction between breast and head is actually a reflection of the much discussed contrast he subsequently draws in the letter between the relative merits of Wordsworth and Milton, whose relevance to *Hyperion* has long been recognized.[6] His deliberations lead him first to assert the primacy of personal experience:

> . . . axioms in philosophy are not axioms until they are proved upon our pulses: We read fine things but never feel them to the full until we have gone the same steps as the Author.—I know this is not plain; you will know exactly my meaning when I say, that now I shall relish Hamlet more than I ever have done—Or, better—You are sensible no man can set down Venery as a bestial or joyless thing until he is sick of it and therefore all philosophizing on it would be mere wording. Until we are sick, we understand not;—in fine, as Byron says, "Knowledge is Sorrow"; and I go on to say that "Sorrow is Wisdom". . . .
>
> (I, 279)

The conjunction of knowledge, sorrow, and wisdom has a clear bearing upon Apollo's dying into life: "Knowledge enormous makes a God of me" (III, 113), and most of that knowledge is sorrowful. Thus Apollo comes to bear the burden of the mystery; the Titans, despite their sickness, cannot understand.

The culmination of thought in this letter to Reynolds is Keats's well-known "simile of human life" as "a large Mansion of Many Apartments, two of which I can only describe, the doors of the rest being as yet shut upon me—":

The first we step into we call the infant or thoughtless Chamber, in which we remain as long as we do not think—We remain there a long while, and notwithstanding the doors of the second Chamber remain wide open, showing a bright appearance, we care not to hasten to it; but are at length imperceptibly impelled by the awakening of the thinking principle—within us—we no sooner get into the second Chamber, which I shall call the Chamber of Maiden-Thought, than we become intoxicated with the light and the atmosphere, we see nothing but pleasant wonders, and think of delaying there for ever in delight: However among the effects this breathing is father of is that tremendous one of sharpening one's vision into the heart and nature of Man—of convincing ones nerves that the World is full of Misery and Heartbreak, Pain, Sickness and oppression—whereby This Chamber of Maiden Thought becomes gradually darken'd and at the same time on all sides of it many doors are set open—but all dark—all leading to dark passages—We see not the ballance of good and evil. We are in a Mist—*We* are now in that state—We feel the "burden of the Mystery." To this point was Wordsworth come, as far as I can conceive when he wrote "Tintern Abbey" and it seems to me that his Genius is explorative of those dark Passages. Now if we live, and go on thinking, we too shall explore them. He is a Genius and superior [to] us, in so far as he can, more than we, make discoveries, and shed a light in them.

(I, 280-81)

The progression from one "Apartment" to the next recalls the stages of aesthetic development outlined in "Sleep and Poetry," with the important difference that the experience which then had been spoken of merely as axioms of artistic progress was now being proved upon his pulses. Exploring the myriad dark passages of life and shedding a light in them was to become the goal of Keats's remaining poetic life, and the saving power of knowledge that those passages contained was to be embodied first in *Hyperion*, a poem about spiritual growth and progress *sub specie aeternitatis*.

"Misery, Heartbreak, Pain, Sickness and oppression"—this is

precisely what Keats encountered upon returning from his Scotch tour in the fall of 1818.[7] Tom's condition had worsened; Keats could read the signs of death. And the poem about Apollo, so long delayed, now became a therapeutic necessity:

> . . . I am obliged to write, and plunge into abstract images to ease myself of [Tom's] countenance his voice and feebleness— so that I live now in a continual fever—it must be poisonous to life although I feel well. Imagine "the hateful siege of contraries"—if I think of fame of poetry it seems a crime to me, and yet I must do so or suffer. . . . I have relapsed into those abstractions *which are my only life.*
>
> (I, 369, 370; italics added)

Poetry would be the means of preserving his own vitality, and as the lines of *Hyperion* steadily accumulated, we hear in the letters a new voice of pride and self-confidence in his poetic achievement. Keats realized that he was setting down verses of great beauty, unlike anything he had written before. It was at this time that he declared to his brother and sister-in-law in America, "I think I shall be among the English Poets after my death; . . . The only thing that can ever affect me personally for more than one short passing day, is any doubt about my powers for poetry—I seldom have any, and I look with hope to the nighing time when I shall have none" (I, 394, 404).

Criticism of *Hyperion* must inevitably focus on the poem's fragmentary state; specifically, we must ask why Keats came to a halt after Apollo's dying into life, one of the most striking episodes of metamorphosis in his poetry. Bate questions whether this climactic event is not "merely an abrupt, not very inventive summary for possible development" and speculates that the lines "were jotted down to get the section off his chest and to provide, to an eye that looked at the poem in its present state, some hint of what lay ahead." Bate is further disturbed that "this fatigued but brisk dispatch through summary" is accompanied by a regression in Book III to the imagery and idiom of *Endymion.*[8] There is much to be said for this view; the last lines do indeed seem rather forced. Still, one must ask why Keats decided to sketch this part of his heroic canvas in precisely this way. Why depict Apollo's rise to full godhood as an event of torturous transformation? Why not, after introducing Apollo, proceed directly to a confrontation between Hyperion and his dispossessor, which would have been a more natural continuation of the narrative line established in Books I and II? Assuming, then, that what Keats did write is in some sense imperfect, we may still try to discover what this seeming divergence from a more expected line of narrative development has to tell us about Keats's thematic intentions in the work. For, indeed, there are subtle indications in the first two books that Keats had envisioned a metamorphic experience for Apollo somewhere in the poem; it may be that only after having written it did he recognize the liability of placing it where he did.

Hyperion constitutes what Keats once said would be his "first Step toward the chief Attempt in the Drama—the playing of different Natures with Joy and Sorrow" (I, 218-19). Despite the graphic physical stasis or constriction of the work (most prominent in books I and II), a moving psychological dynamism permeates each of the poem's carefully drawn scenes; and, as Bate notes, "a full 58 per cent of the lines of the first two books consist of dialogue." [9] More specifically, the dialogue consists largely of questions and answers—the interrogative mode accounts for much of the poem's dramatic effect. Questioning is the means whereby the central figures—Saturn, Hyperion, and Apollo—try to release the tension generated by bewilderment, which, significantly, afflicts both the defeated and the triumphant race. But the crucial difference between the Titans' and Apollo's questioning is that whereas Mnemosyne's knowing "response" dispels the new god's "aching ignorance" and brings about his metamorphosis to full divinity, Oceanus' "eternal truth" has no transforming effect upon the lamenting Titans; if anything, it exacerbates their plight.

The diction and imagery of the poem make clear that virtually all the characters are in some sense *sick;* only Apollo can be cured:

> Deep in the shady sadness of a vale
> Far sunken from the healthy breath of morn,
> Far from the fiery noon, and eve's one star,

> Sat grey-hair'd Saturn, quiet as a stone,
> (5) Still as the silence round about his lair;
> Forest on forest hung about his head
> Like cloud on cloud. No stir of air was there,
> Not so much life as on a summer's day
> Robs not one light seed from the feather'd grass,
> (10) But where the dead leaf fell, there did it rest.
> A stream went voiceless by, still deadened more
> By reason of his fallen divinity
> Spreading a shade: the Naiad 'mid her reeds
> Press'd her cold finger closer to her lips.

Saturn's lair is a vast sickroom. Its claustrophobic forests and withering vegetation, its dead air and chill, "voiceless" streams make it the reverse of the easeful, vitalizing Keatsian bower so familiar in his previous poetry. The sequence of images, as elsewhere in the poem, is cinematic, ending with the marvelously evocative closeup of the naiad, with its delicately poised, almost evanescent verticals: the reeds and the single finger lifted in admonition (patient sleeping; do not disturb).

> (15) Along the margin-sand large foot-marks went,
> No further than to where his feet had stray'd,
> And slept there since. Upon the sodden ground
> His old right hand lay nerveless, listless, dead,
> Unsceptred; and his realmless eyes were closed;
> (20) While his bow'd head seem'd list'ning to the Earth,
> His ancient mother, for some comfort yet.

The synecdoches of lines 15-21, moving deliberately from foot to head, sum up Saturn's plight: he is a shattered being. Similarly, the somber procession of epithets—"nerveless, listless, dead, / Unsceptred"—ironically underscores the sovereign's vanished majesty. When "at length old Saturn lifted up / His faded eyes, and saw his kingdom gone, / And all the gloom and sorrow of the place," he "then spake, / As with a palsied tongue, and while his beard / Shook horrid with such aspen-malady" (I, 89-91, 92-94). When he bitterly proclaims his calamity, the effort merely excites his disease:

"This passion lifted him upon his feet, / And made his hands to struggle in the air, / His Druid locks to shake and ooze with sweat, / His eyes to fever out, his voice to cease" (I, 135-38).

Thea, wife of Hyperion, is similarly afflicted. She is statuesque in form, "But oh! how unlike marble was that face: / How beautiful, if sorrow had not made / Sorrow more beautiful than Beauty's self" (I, 34-36)—the first of several images in the poem whereby Keats moves the Titans toward the condition of mortality. Her presence with Saturn in the lair is an inversion of Peona's with Endymion in their island arbor (I, 407-35ff.), for whereas Endymion's magic sleep there calmed him to life again, enabling him to open "his eyelids with a healthier brain" (I, 465), Saturn's sleep yields no refreshment and Thea's nursing can have no effect:

"Saturn, look up—though wherefore, poor old King?
I have no comfort for thee, no not one:
I cannot say, 'O wherefore sleepest thou?'
For heaven is parted from thee, and the earth
Knows thee not, thus afflicted, for a God."

                                                                        (I, 52-56)

Distraught from the " 'weary griefs' " of this " 'aching time' " (I, 64, 66), Thea must endure the shattered monarch's obsessive, almost childlike questioning of his unmerited fate.[10] Like Keats atop Ben Nevis, he is shrouded in the mist of ignorance; Saturn's primitive "world of thought and mental might" yields no enlightenment ("Read me a lesson, Muse," 14). Futilely he implores Thea:

"Look up, and tell me if this feeble shape
Is Saturn's; tell me, if thou hear'st the voice
Of Saturn; tell me, if this wrinkling brow,
Naked and bare of its great diadem,
Peers like the front of Saturn. Who had power
To make me desolate? whence came the strength?
How was it nurtur'd to such bursting forth,
While Fate seem'd strangled in my nervous grasp?"

                                                                        (I, 98-105)

Most piteous, and thematically most relevant, is Saturn's loss of creative power. In a fit of self-delusion, he declares that " 'there shall be / Beautiful things made new, for the surprise / Of the sky children; I will give command' ":

> "But cannot I create?
> Cannot I form? Cannot I fashion forth
> Another world, another universe,
> To overbear and crumble this to nought?
> Where is another Chaos? Where?"
> (I, 131-33, 141-45)

But precisely the power of creation is destined for Apollo, whose deification symbolizes his acquiring full poetic mastery as the father of all verse; whereas Saturn's fate is to wither into inertia amid the chaos occasioned by his conqueror's triumph. Of course, if Saturn *could* fashion forth another world, he would thereby transform his woeful condition. But the defeat is immutable; *he* cannot die into a new life of sovereignty. This is made explicit by some lines in Keats's manuscript omitted in the printed version of the poem:

> Thus the old Eagle drowsy with great grief
> Sat moulting his weak Plumage never more
> To be restored or soar against the Sun. . . .[11]

The hopelessness of the Titans' plight, so movingly expressed by Saturn's unanswered questioning, is summed up in a lovely touch of dramatic irony at the end of this scene. His deluded call for "another chaos" rises to Olympus and "made quake / The rebel three"—his dispossessing sons Jupiter, Neptune, and Pluto (I, 146-47). Thea is momentarily, and mistakenly, encouraged by the distant rumble: " 'This cheers our fallen house' " (I, 150).

The scene then shifts from Saturn's dark vale to Hyperion's blazing palace. This change of locale is accompanied by an intensification of Keats's concern with the psychology of defeat, which he achieves through a subtle change in technique. The images of Saturn and Thea were primarily visual, creating a series of tableaus (at one point Keats describes the two figures as "postured motion-less, / Like natural sculpture in cathedral cavern" [I, 85-86]). The sequence of more or less static pictures was appropriate for charac-ters whose spiritual crisis is circumscribed because fully experi-enced. Hyperion, by contrast, is nearly always in motion; his restlessness suggests his imminent political and psychological col-lapse. Unlike the other Titans, he "still kept / His sov'reignty, and rule, and majesty," but he is "unsecure," haunted by "omens drear," "horrors, portion'ed to a giant nerve" which "Oft made Hyperion ache" (I, 164-65, 168, 169, 175-76). Though the point cannot be pressed too far, this shift in Keats's narrative focus from Saturn and Thea's physical inertia (symbolizing spiritual hopeless-ness) to Hyperion's restless mental torment ironically reflects the poem's central dramatic premise, namely, the shift in sovereignty from those of material power to those of tormented yet com-prehending mind, Keats's prophetic reading of contemporary his-tory. In his troubled mobility, and dreadfully aware of a defeat he refuses to accept, Hyperion is a transition figure between the para-lyzed, vanquished Saturn and the free-ranging, ultimately trium-phant Apollo. Of course, Hyperion is also, and more pertinently, Apollo's counterpart in the old order, for whereas the new god will soon be metamorphosed into a full-fledged celestial power, the brooding, restless Titan is in the process of losing his grip.

Keats depicts Hyperion's anxiety not only through his restless-ness (instead of relaxing at sunset, "He pac'd away the pleasant hours of ease / With stride colossal" [I, 194-95]), but also through alterations in his sensory awareness:

Also, when he would taste the spicy wreaths
Of incense, breath'd aloft from sacred hills,
Instead of sweets, his ample palate took
Savour of poisonous brass and metal sick:
(I, 186-89)

Similarly, instead of seeing his realm as the hot, lucent empire it is, Hyperion is beset with chilling hallucinatory omens, projections of his sense of imminent disaster:

"O dreams of day and night!
O monstrous forms! O effigies of pain!
O spectres busy in a cold, cold gloom!
O lank-eared Phantoms of black-weeded pools!
Why do I know ye? why have I seen ye? why
Is my eternal essence thus distraught
To see and to behold these horrors new?
Saturn is fallen, am I too to fall?

Am I to leave this haven of my rest,
This cradle of my glory, this soft clime,
This calm luxuriance of blissful light,
These crystalline pavilions, and pure fanes,
Of all my lucent empire? It is left
Deserted, void, nor any haunt of mine.
The blaze, the splendour and the symmetry,
I cannot see—but darkness, death and darkness."

                                    (I, 227-42)

Hyperion's desperate questioning, like Saturn's, fades into the chill, pestilent air of defeat; when he swears vengeance on " 'that infant thunderer, rebel Jove,' " the dreadful hallucinatory forms gather into "A mist . . . as from a scummy march" (I, 249, 258). All he can know is a vague but certain foreboding of doom. Hyperion's fury finds provisional, that is ironic, release in a convulsive fit, which clearly prefigures Apollo's wild commotions as he dies into life; but for Hyperion there can be no such metamorphosis; the spasm is merely physical:

At this, through all his bulk an agony
Crept gradual, from the feet unto the crown,
Like a lithe serpent vast and muscular
Making slow way, with head and neck convuls'd
From over-strained might.
                                    (I, 259-63)

In a pathetic gesture of compensation for his imminent over-throw, Hyperion tries to make the sun rise six hours before its appointed time. This is analogous to Saturn's longing to fashion forth another world:

> Fain would he have commanded, fain took throne
> And bid the day begin, if but for change.
> He might not:—No, though a primeval God:
> The sacred seasons might not be disturb'd.
> Therefore the operations of the dawn
> Stay'd in their birth, even as here 'tis told.
>
> (I, 290-95)

"If but for change." An alteration of natural law, a new cosmic cycle, would mean the transformation of Hyperion's dread into security; instead, "the bright Titan, phrenzied with new woes, / Unus'd to bend, by hard compulsion bent / His spirit to the sorrow of the time" (I, 299-301). The hitherto restless sun-deity is now prostrate: "He stretch'd himself in grief and radiance faint," unwittingly imitating Saturn asleep on the sodden ground (I, 304).

In Book I Saturn and Hyperion vainly long for metamorphoses that would reinvest them with their former power. In Book II they learn why such a reversal is impossible. Oceanus' speech is bitter medicine indeed, because while it celebrates the inevitability of change, it makes clear the Titans' limited role in the cosmic process—they can only change for the worse. Therefore the fallen Titans' meeting place, "this nest of pain" (II, 90), is as dark as Saturn's sickroom / vale, though without its merciful silence; filled with groans and "the solid roar / Of thunderous waterfalls and torrents hoarse" (II, 7-8), this new den is part torture chamber, part funeral parlor.

The action of Book II opens with the arrival of Saturn and closes with that of Hyperion. Neither is to any avail. Sunk in despair, Saturn endures a living death, "for Fate / Had pour'd a mortal oil upon his head, / A disanointing poison" (II, 96-98). His speech to the prostrate Titans, again filled with vain questioning, protests his ignorance. His sources of knowledge have proved useless: neither in " 'the legends of the first of days' " nor in the signs and portents of natural elements " 'Can I find reason why ye should be thus' " (II, 132, 149). He appeals to Oceanus, in whose face he sees " 'astonied, that severe content / Which comes of thought and musing' " (II,

165-66). Oceanus' authority in explaining the Titans' defeat is more comprehensive than the individual operations of nature; it is nature's law itself:

> "Yet listen, ye who will, whilst I bring proof
> How ye, perforce, must be content to stoop:
> And in the proof much comfort will I give,
> If ye will take that comfort in its truth.
> We fall by course of Nature's law, not force
> Of thunder, or of Jove. Great Saturn, thou
> Hast sifted well the atom-universe;
> But for this reason, that thou art the King,
> And only blind from sheer supremacy,
> One avenue was shaded from thine eyes,
> Through which I wandered to eternal truth.
> And first, as thou wast not the first of powers,
> So art thou not the last; it cannot be:
> Thou art not the beginning nor the end."
>   (II, 177-90)

Oceanus' theodicy is resolutely unchristian, denying the alpha and omega of orthodoxy. Rather, in his review of the creation of the universe, the imagery is of potentially endless cycles of birth, growth, and ripening, and also of a gradual refinement of life-forms, expressed in metaphors denoting a progressive upward movement:

>   Say, doth the dull soil
> Quarrel with the proud forests it hath fed,
> And feedeth still, more comely than itself?
> Can it deny the chiefdom of green groves?
> Or shall the tree be envious of the dove
> Because it cooeth, and hath snowy wings
> To wander wherewithal and find its joys?
> We are such forest-trees, and our fair boughs
> Have bred forth, not pale solitary doves,
> But eagles golden-feather'd, who do tower
> Above us in their beauty, and must reign
> In right thereof; for 'tis the eternal law

That first in beauty should be first in might:
Yea, by that law, another race may drive
Our conquerors to mourn as we do now.
                              (II, 217-31)

Oceanus accepts the inevitable metamorphoses of power in the
cosmos, to which personal loss or gain is irrelevant. Nature's law is
severe, although Oceanus does not acknowledge this overtly;
rather, it emerges through the imperative, somewhat pompous
tone of the speech (established by words like "proof," "perforce,"
and especially the reiterated "must"). Such a tone is, of course,
appropriate to the hard subject, but it also serves to qualify
Oceanus' wisdom and prepares us for the voices of Clymene and
Enceladus, which follow. She is the helpless, ravished listener, he
the useless rager; the music Clymene makes (and the lovelier music
she hears—Apollo crying his own name) is counterpointed by Enceladus' gruff noise of revenge. The authenticity of their responses
to defeat also qualifies Oceanus' lofty stoicism, though without
really subverting it. The effect is dramatic, "the playing of different Natures with Joy and Sorrow."

Hyperion's theatrical appearance at the book's close is a false
dawn; that is, his approaching light signifies no new day for the
Titans but, rather, harshly illuminates the disaster of their immediate past in all its immutability:

In pale and silver silence they remain'd,
Till suddenly a splendour, like the morn,
Pervaded all the beetling gloomy steeps,
All the sad spaces of oblivion. . . .

It was Hyperion:—a granite peak
His bright feet touch'd, and there he stay'd to view
The misery his brilliance had betray'd
To the most hateful seeing of itself.
                              (II, 356-59, 367-70)

The scene's final event is more brutally ironic than Thea's mistak-
ing the heavenly rumble at the end of Book I. Enceladus and his

wrathful cohorts shout Saturn's name, and Hyperion echoes it from his peak. But this shouting is merely a travesty of Apollo's blissfully melodious crying of his own name, which had made Clymene "sick / Of joy and grief at once" (II, 288-89). The name of Saturn issues from "hollow throats" (II, 391).

The transition from the Titans in Books I and II to Apollo in Book III could not be more sharply drawn. The false dawn of Hyperion gives way to the appearance of Apollo at "morning twilight" (III, 33), the propitious time for metamorphosis. The chill, moribund dens of the Titans are succeeded by Apollo's Delian bower, flushed with vitality: "let faint-lipp'd shells, / On sands, or in great deeps, vermilion turn / Through all their labyrinths; and let the maid / Blush keenly, as with some warm kiss surpris'd" (III, 19-22). Having completed the drama of the Titans' irreversible fate, Keats turns to "loveliness new born"; Apollo is all potentiality (III, 79).

Yet like his forebears, Apollo is himself filled with questions in his dialogue with Mnemosyne, the Titaness who has forsaken "old and sacred thrones" to nurse Apollo in his infancy and to supervise his assumption to full divinity (III, 77). She alone among the Titans adheres to Oceanus' counsel to bear all naked truths and to envision circumstance all calm (Apollo notes the " 'eternal calm' " in Mnemosyne's eyes [III, 60]). Thus both the new god's questioning and Mnemosyne herself serve as bridges between the old and the new and suggest deep continuities between them, which Apollo's metamorphosis will confirm. For part of its torturous effect derives from his comprehending the pain that his own triumph has necessarily caused.

Some of Apollo's questioning is merely rhetorical. When Mnemosyne encourages him to " 'Explain thy griefs,' " he declares: " 'Why should I tell thee what thou so well seest? / Why should I strive to show what from thy lips / Would come no mystery?' " (III, 84-86). At other times he can partly answer his own perplexity through the intuition of dreaming:

"How cam'st thou over the unfooted sea?
Or hath that antique mien and robed form
Mov'd in these vales invisible till now?

Sure I have heard those vestments sweeping o'er
The fallen leaves, when I have sat alone
In cool mid-forest. Surely I have traced
The rustle of those ample skirts about
These grassy solitudes, and seen the flowers
Lift up their heads, as still the whisper pass'd.
Goddess! I have beheld those eyes before,
And their eternal calm, and all that face,
Or I have dream'd."

(III, 50-61)

But the answers to other questions he cannot as yet divine:

"O why should I
Feel curs'd and thwarted, when the liegeless air
Yields to my step aspirant? why should I
Spurn the green turf as hateful to my feet?
Goddess benign, point forth some unknown thing:
Are there not other regions than this isle?
What are the stars?"
"Where is power?
Whose hand, whose essence, what divinity
Makes this alarum in the elements,
While I here idle listen on the shores
In fearless yet in aching ignorance?"

(III, 91-97, 103-7)

Like the Titans, Apollo is bewildered because he is ignorant; but unlike theirs, his discontented state is metamorphosed because he can absorb—not merely listen to—proffered knowledge. He reads in Mnemosyne's face the great lesson that always marks the transition from adolescence to adulthood, the lesson that Keats had struggled with during the long months of anxiety and death that prepared him finally to write his poem; he learns, that is, the tragedy inherent in all process, the inevitability of *dying* into life:

"Mute thou remainest—mute! yet I can read
A wondrous lesson in thy silent face:

Knowledge enormous makes a God of me.
Names, deeds, gray legends, dire events, rebellions,
Majesties, sovran voices, agonies,
Creations and destroyings, all at once
Pour into the wide hollows of my brain,
And deify me, as if some blithe wine
Or bright elixir peerless I had drunk,
And so become immortal."—Thus the God,
While his enkindled eyes, with level glance
Beneath his white soft temples, stedfast kept
Trembling with light upon Mnemosyne.
Soon wild commotions shook him, and made flush
All the immortal fairness of his limbs;
Most like the struggle at the gate of death;
Or liker still to one who should take leave
Of pale immortal death, and with a pang
As hot as death's is chill, with fierce convulse
Die into life: so young Apollo anguish'd:
His very hair, his golden tresses famed,
Kept undulation round his eager neck.
During the pain Mnemosyne upheld
Her arms as one who prophesied.—At length
Apollo shriek'd; and lo! from all his limbs
Celestial   *   *   *   *   *   *   *   *   *   *

*   *   *   *   *   *   *   *   *   *   *   *   *

(III, 111-36)

Before dismissing this as a mere sketch, we should at least note
Keats's attempt to be comprehensive, that is, to render Apollo's
metamorphosis both from without and within. The inrush of tragic
history (it is really, as Harold Bloom says, mythology [12]) effects the
disturbance of ordinary consciousness common to all Keatsian
metamorphoses, here likened to drunkenness. Admittedly, the metaphoric description is too brief. What seems lacking is any notice of
the frightening mental havoc that extreme "intoxication" produces; instead, Apollo's sense of pain is for the most part observed

externally, which makes it somewhat less affecting than it might have been. The wild commotions and the fierce convulse are authentic, but instead of fully participating in Apollo's agony we are kept somewhat at a distance. Still, the pressure of Keats's language is intense, driven to extremes. His own triumphant wresting with similitudes—"Most like the struggle at the gate of death; / Or liker still to one who should take leave / Of pale immortal death, and with a pang / As hot as death's is chill"—provides a precise poetic equivalent to Apollo's agonized rise to supremacy. If Keats's description of the new god's anguish borders on the grotesque, as has been charged, it is because it cannot be otherwise. Such crises of transition are never refined.

Apollo's deathlike struggle, which transcends death, is in fact a rebirth: his inchoate or "Perplex'd" self dies, giving birth to a new divine consciousness. The sequence of events in this episode obviously follows the metamorphosis pattern, with its cycle of discontent (here, the god's aching ignorance), a lapse of ordinary consciousness (Apollo's sense of inebriation, followed by the convulsions), and finally the emergence of a new self (his full divinity). Clearly, the transformation is caused by his becoming convinced that *inevitably and necessarily* the "World is full of Misery and Heartbreak, Pain, Sickness and oppression." This hard knowledge is what makes him mightier than the Titans; his superior beauty is merely a sign of his knowing.

There can be little doubt as to what Apollo's metamorphosis signified for Keats personally. It denotes his sense of having arrived at the first stage of creative maturity through the difficult but morally necessary acceptance of the tragic vision, which would henceforth inform his best poetry. That is, the beauty of his verse would be of greater amplitude than before, because it would comprehend a wider spectrum of the light and shade in human existence. Unfortunately, however, under the pressure of expressing this personal sense of attainment, *Hyperion* breaks off. One explanation of this may be that the hopeful political allegory of a new order replacing an outmoded regime, which the narrative was designed in part to support, had become subverted by the introspective symbolism of the Keatsian persona's triumph. Any return to the severe epic grandeur of the poem's first two books would probably have appeared anticlimactic and stylistically dissonant, for as Douglas Bush has noted, "the wedding of Miltonic technique to Wordsworthian inwardness was almost bound to be an unequal union." [13] But whatever its shortcomings, *Hyperion* is Keats's declaration of faith in the possibility of spiritual growth through the forthright scrutiny of human crises. The poem acknowledges the tragic irony inherent in all change, as well as the incomprehension that such change can generate; but it also asserts that an understanding of this irony empowers one to endure it and finally to survive it.

Unquestionably, Keats had become a different person since the days of *Endymion,* and this is nowhere more clearly revealed than in the quality of the metamorphoses that climax each poem. For whereas *Endymion's* apotheosis was merely implied, with no indication of its being at all stressful (though the Cave of Quietude hints at what might have been), Apollo's transformation is a convulsive agony, driving him perilously close to self-extinction even as his soul marshals its forces to emerge reborn. Yet despite this important difference, the dénouements of both poems are unsatisfying, though for diverse reasons. At the close of *Endymion,* the hero's matured understanding and appreciation of love are not only undramatized; they are not even voiced. Only the struggle for their attainment seems to have interested Keats, so that the poem must end with the lovers' union and escape. Similarly, in *Hyperion,* Apollo's new tragic awareness must be accepted largely on faith; his metamorphosis is a convincing assertion of such awareness, but its effect upon him is not clarified through subsequent action. This points up the epistemological nature of both poems. They are distillations of Keats's knowledge composed more or less while the learning process was taking place.

Most of the poems that follow *Endymion* and *Hyperion,* however, are of a rather different sort. They are more fully dramatic and aesthetically more coherent because they utilize the knowledge Keats gained from writing these earlier works. Thus in many ways *The Eve of St. Agnes* is the poet's reworking of *Endymion,* and the differences between them are a striking measure of his artistic and emotional maturing. Similarly, the tragic awareness that Keats, through Apollo, merely asserted in *Hyperion,* subsequently animates the great odes of the coming spring. In both *The Eve of St. Agnes* and "Ode to a Nightingale" metamorphosis figures prominently. It is to these poems that I now wish to turn.

Notes

1. For the most complete discussion of Keats's aims in *Hyperion,* see Sperry, *Keats the Poet,* pp. 155-59, in particular his comments on how the poem reflects "The sense of loss, endemic to the times" (pp. 157-58). Kenneth Muir's essay, "The Meaning of 'Hyperion'," in *John Keats: A Reassessment,* ed. Kenneth Muir (Liverpool: Liverpool Univ. Press, 1958), pp. 103-23, contains the best account of the poem's political implications.
2. Sperry, *Keats the Poet,* p. 155.
3. Ward, *John Keats: The Making of a Poet,* p. 218.
4. "During a year of 'purgatory blind,' when every day his conception of poetry and his knowledge of the function and destiny of the poet changed, and his own instant knowledge of the mystery the poet had to comprehend was deepened, he became reluctant to begin this poem beyond all others" (John Middleton Murry, *Keats and Shakespeare* [London, 1925], p. 80).
5. Ward notes that "perhaps without quite realizing it, he was developing a vivid sense of the human comedy with its many-sided clash of differing natures, which he now began watching with the same detached pleasure as he would a play . . ." (*John Keats: The Making of a Poet,* p. 155).
6. For a discussion of how Keats conceived of Milton and Wordsworth as both moral and aesthetic models, and how they diversely influenced the composition of *Hyperion,* see Bate, *John Keats,* pp. 321-35, and Sperry, *Keats the Poet,* pp. 158-79. The latter's fine account of *The Excursion* is especially revealing.
7. Although the principal legacy of Keats's northern tour was his absorbing "the intellect the countenance" of the Lake District, his rapture at new sights became increasingly shadowed by unanticipated scenes of human squalor and degradation (especially in Scotland and Ireland), as well as by his own physical discomfort. It is a question whether Keats and Brown left Ireland because of the exorbitant expense of traveling there or because of the infamous "Duchess of Dunghill," the depraved old woman carried about on a litter, who epitomized for Keats the filth of Irish peasant life. Their subsequent walk across the Isle of Mull was "wretched," engendering the ominous sore throat which was to cut short Keats's tour. Food and lodging were monotonously bad. Worst of all, the manly test of scaling Ben Nevis left Keats feeling not triumphant but hopelessly perplexed. The climb was deceptively arduous, the descent "most vile," the summit obfuscated: ". . . all my eye doth meet / Is mist and crag, not only on this height, / But in the world of thought and mental might!" ("Read me a lesson, Muse," 12-14). See *Letters,* I, 298-360.
8. Bate, *John Keats,* pp. 406, 403.

9. Ibid., p. 391.

10. His fate is unmerited, of course, because he has done nothing evil; on the contrary, Keats calls attention repeatedly to the benevolence of the Titans' reign. Saturn laments that he is " 'smother'd up, / And buried from all godlike exercise / Of influence benign on planets pale, / Of admonitions to the winds and seas, / Of peaceful sway above man's harvesting, / And all those acts which Deity supreme / Doth ease its heart of love in' " (I, 106-12). The Titans' frustrating attempt to deal with undeserved loss reflects Keats's own circumstances; as Bate notes, "The question [of confronting the hurt of loss] had been familiar to Keats since the age of eight" (*John Keats,* p. 398).

11. *Keats: The Complete Poems,* ed. M. Allott, p. 398n.

12. Harold Bloom, *The Visionary Company* (Garden City, N.Y.: Doubleday Anchor Books, 1961), p. 416.

13. Douglas Bush, *Mythology and the Romantic Tradition in English Poetry* (New York: W. W. Norton, 1963), p. 119.

4.

The Eve of St. Agnes: The Honey'd Middle of the Night

The Eve of St. Agnes is the most transparent of Keats's narrative poems, and yet perhaps for this very reason it has aroused widely differing critical responses. Long regarded as merely a beautiful tapestry devoid of meaning, during the last twenty-five years the poem has been discussed, as Sperry notes, "with a certain grim intellectual seriousness," which may strike the reader as oversubtle or forced.[1] Such commentary is laudable insofar as it challenges the claim that the poem is mindless; but, as is usually the case with reactive criticism, it tends to lose a sense of the whole, however suggestive it may be about particular details. Misplaced emphasis, I would argue, has subverted much of the recent discussion of *St. Agnes,* which is, quite simply, a finely wrought dramatic tale about falling in love.[2]

We do well to bear in mind Bate's cautious description of *The Eve of St. Agnes* as "a less ambitious poem in a different form" from that of Keats's current major project, *Hyperion.* Written in late January 1818 (that is, between books II and III of *Hyperion*), its luxurious sensuousness, as well as its predominantly joyous tone, mark

64

it as a relief, even a release, from his grave brooding on the Titans' fall.[3] I believe we can call *St. Agnes* a relatively minor poem if our perspective is governed by Keats's overall poetic goals. His own comments on it reflect a noteworthy sense of proportion. In a letter to Taylor about "the writing of a few fine Plays—my greatest ambition," Keats says that he wishes "to diffuse the colouring of St. Agnes eve throughout a Poem in which Character and Sentiment would be the figures to such drapery" (II, 234). We should not, of course, interpret this to mean that he felt the poem to be lacking in character development and emotional resonance but, rather, that they are insufficiently rounded and distinct, too bound up with the coloring, the drapery. Similarly, Keats laments that, like *Isabella* (though to a lesser extent), the poem is "too smokeable" (i.e., easily derided): "There is too much inexperience of life, and simplicity of knowledge in it" (II, 174)—which is not to say that the poem is devoid of psychological interest, but that its truths are partial because of its somewhat limited emotional range. "There is no objection of this kind to Lamia," a poem in which love not only blossoms but wilts.

Keats's comments on *St. Agnes* are instructive not simply for their critical acuity and deliberate modesty but because they en-courage us to focus, however critically, on matters of drama, not metaphysics. This is important when we consider, for example, the scene in which Madeline half-awakens from her blissful dream of Porphyro and, glimpsing her real lover, experiences a "painful change":

> "And those sad eyes were spiritual and clear:
> How chang'd thou art! how pallid, chill, and drear!
> Give me that voice again, my Porphyro,
> Those looks immortal, those complainings dear!"
>
> (310-14)

Thinking back to *Endymion,* and more importantly forward to the odes and *Lamia,* we are tempted to seize upon the incident as an important expression of Keats's concern with the rival claims of the ideal and the real. Unquestionably, that theme does enter the poem, but it is not at all its major preoccupation. As Bate observes, the dramatic context of the poem permits Keats merely to note (but not to explore in depth) "one relatively simple but recurring thought . . . which is to become more prominent in the poetry of 1819: a dream—like innocence—cannot be lived in the world without being violated; and yet, whatever is lost, actual happiness is impossible without an awakening from dream to reality." [4] I would further argue that Madeline's half-awakening, and what follows it, have primary relevance to Keats's unfolding psychology of love per se, and not to love as a symbol for any metaphysical scheme.[5]

To repeat, then, *The Eve of St. Agnes* is first of all a poem about the experience of falling in love, and there can be little doubt that its real source is Keats's affection for Fanny Brawne. We need to remind ourselves of the obvious—that the poem is, as Ward says "Keats's 'Epithalamion' in narrative form, celebrating the joys of a first love fulfilled in a runaway marriage." Noting echoes in the poem of the whole range of Keats's reading, particularly of *Romeo and Juliet,* she rightly stresses "the poetic intention at the front of his mind which called up the words and images from his memory— the felt emotion, the actual experience, the sense of reality which he wished to express." [6] Keats set his playful yet elegant marriage song in the world of medieval romance for two related reasons. First, by embracing the diverse charms of that literary mode (as well as engagingly mocking those aspects of it that he had come to regard as saccharine [7]), he could indulge freely his natural poetic love of the sensuous, thereby creating an idealized yet credible ambience for his story of love's consummation. And second, by distancing the tale in time, he sought to achieve what he considered the requisite ethereal effect whereby he might paradoxically both modulate and intensify the expression of his erotic desire, the true energy of his inspiration. "I have loved the principle of beauty in all things," Keats wrote Fanny at the start of his last struggle (II, 263); nowhere in his work is this more fully felt than in *The Eve of St. Agnes.*

The dramatic premise of the poem, of course, is the superstition of St. Agnes's Eve, whereby a maiden might see her future husband in a dream if she performed certain rites, namely fasting and lying rigidly in bed—"Nor look behind, nor sideways, but require / Of heaven with upward eyes for all that they desire" (53-54). Interestingly, *St. Agnes* is preoccupied from start to finish with performing rituals of various sorts. If we stand back and take a panoramic view of the poem's action, we find that it consists of praying, of reveling, of seducing, of lovemaking; and it points toward another set of rituals—domesticating: Porphyro eventually promises Madeline that " 'o'er the southern moors I have a home for thee' " (351). Moreover, the quality of each of these rituals establishes a significant progression. We move from ones in which passion has been diverted to nonvital ends (the ancient Beadsman's abstemious praying "among / Rough ashes" [25-26] and the revelers' hedonism) to social rites of increasing vitality and worth. Seen in this way, Madeline and Porphyro's sexual union grows out of moribund asceticism and a gradually refined hedonism to emerge as the most fully vitalizing of human activities. Moreover, just as in *Hyperion* Apollo's rise to full divinity was dependent upon his absorption of the experience of his predecessors, so does the lovemaking of Madeline and Porphyro in *St. Agnes* incorporate aspects of the rituals that it ultimately transcends. In order to see how this is so, we must examine each of the poem's rituals in turn.

The poem begins in an atmosphere of numbing cold, severely restricted movement, and silence, which spares no living thing:

> St. Agnes' Eve—Ah, bitter chill it was!
> The owl, for all his feathers, was a-cold;
> The hare limp'd trembling through the frozen grass,
> And silent was the flock in woolly fold:
> Numb were the Beadsman's fingers, while he told
> His rosary, and while his frosted breath,
> Like Pious incense from a censer old,
> Seem'd taking flight for heaven, without a death,
> Past the sweet Virgin's picture, while his prayer he saith.
>
> (1-9)

The first ritual we encounter is the most solitary—communion between a penitent and his God. For Keats it is also the most life-denying; the Beadsman's tactile sense is impaired, his spirit a mere cloud of evanescent breath (as in old pictures of the dying; "without a death" is a local irony shortly confirmed in stanza II—"already had his deathbell rung"—and at the poem's conclusion). "Meagre, barefoot, wan," the Beadsman passes through a chapel aisle of "The sculptur'd dead" who "seem to freeze, / Emprison'd in black, purgatorial rails" (12, 14-15), reminding us of the vanquished Saturn and Thea "postured motionless, / Like natural sculpture in cathedral cavern; / The frozen God still couchant on the earth" (I, 85-87). The Beadsman even seems to have become incapable of sympathy for his kind: as he passes by the sculptured dead, "his weak spirit fails / To think how they may ache in icy hoods and mails" (17-18). This is in the most telling contrast to Porphyro's melting into Madeline's dream, "as the rose / Blendeth its odour with the violet" (320-21), at the poem's climax. Though the Beadsman's intense observance evidences a passionate nature, his energy has been wasted in solitude, and his enfeebled form seems to dissolve in the rough ashes of his penance, just as his frosted breath vanishes into the night air.

Keats dismisses this useless creature (in an omitted stanza he tells the reader, flippantly, to "Give him a tear" [8]) and turns for contrast to the mass of guests in the adjoining banquet hall.[9] Unlike the Beadsman's, their rites are social and hedonistic—an "argent revelry" (37) of dancing, carousing, gossiping, and seducing (Madeline is approached, in vain, by "many a tiptoe, amorous cavalier" [60]). Keats's judgment of this "throng'd resort / Of whisperers in anger, or in sport" who exchange "looks of love, defiance, hate, and scorn" (67-69) is almost as unsparing as that of the Beadsman. They are characterized mainly through the boisterous, brassy music that accompanies their meaningless pleasures: "the silver, snarling trumpets 'gan to chide" (31). "Numerous as shadows haunting fairily / The brain, new stuff'd, in youth, with triumphs gay / Of old romance," this adolescent crowd is also easily dismissed: "These let us wish away" (39-41).[10]

But while Keats may invite us to wish away these observers of contrasted yet equally empty rituals, he does not want us to forget them; indeed, the Beadsman's self-denial has its analogue in Madeline's decision to observe the rites of St. Agnes's Eve, while Porphyro appears *at first* as merely another whisperer in anger or in sport, a tiptoe amorous cavalier bent on seduction. The protagonists, however, do not simply echo the ideas sounded contrapuntally in the poem's prelude; rather, their actions develop and refine both the spiritual and the physical into forms that are humanly meaningful, thereby permitting them to be harmonized at the poem's climactic moment. *St. Agnes's* narrative development is indeed musical, even to including an extended coda and bold final chords; and the transformations in the characters of Porphyro and Madeline (who, of course, dramatize the refinement and blending of the poem's principal motifs) are akin to the subtle chromatic changes in music.

The personalities of Madeline and Porphyro emerge less through what they say or do than through the tone of the narrator's observations of them. Keats's sureness of phrasing and command of versification, so notable in *Hyperion,* are also evident in *St. Agnes;* but in addition there is now a finely tuned, quicksilver flexibility in the language, which produces delicately etched psychological portraits of the protagonists (this flexibility will serve Keats well in the dialectical lyrics he is to write within the next few months). For example, the initial description of Madeline makes clear that her observance of the rites of St. Agnes's Eve is solipsistic and therefore naïve, but the narrator regards her self-deceptive retreat into dreams with a subtle blend of tenderness and gentle admonition. His attitude is almost parental as he watches her drift toward the ineluctable sexual initiation, sympathetic to both her ardor and her adolescent need to cloak it in dream-rites, yet at the same time realistically aware of the dream's inadequacy and of Madeline's need to realize this as well. By turns indulgent and coercive, he notes but does not exploit the somewhat ludicrous side of her behavior. Above all, the narrator's tone is comic, for he is celebrating the most joyous of natural processes, a young girl's emergence into full womanhood.

Thus the narrator bids us "turn, sole-thoughted, to one Lady there, / Whose heart had brooded, all that wintry day, / On love, and wing'd St. Agnes' saintly care, / As she had heard old dames full many times declare" (42-45). "Brooded," with its disparate psychological and biological connotations, catches Madeline's mental state exactly: like an anxious hen warming her egg, she moodily anticipates her night of dreaming and the truth that is supposed to arise from it. The redundancy of "St. Agnes' saintly care" slyly reveals the urgency of Madeline's faith in what can be taken seriously only by aging gossips and inexperienced girls.[11] "Full of this whim was thoughtful Madeline" (55): the candid noun renders the subsequent epithet smilingly ironic. Like the Beadsman contemplating the Virgin's picture, Madeline is isolated by her reverie: "her maiden eyes divine, / Fix'd on the floor, saw many a sweeping train / Pass by—she heeded not at all"; oblivious to actual suitors, "her heart was otherwhere: / She sigh'd for Agnes' dreams, the sweetest of the year" (57-59, 62-63). Her sigh is but one of many gestures that reveal her incipient sexual excitement: "She danc'd along with vague, regardless eyes, / Anxious her lips, her breathing quick and short: / The hallow'd hour was near at hand" (64-66). The interplay of "hallow'd hour" with the physicality of the preceding images makes the lines wink with irony; she is not so different from the amorous cavaliers she ignores. In short, Madeline is an adorable hypocrite: "So, purposing each moment to retire, / She linger'd still" (73-74). The heroine's discontent, like that of so many Keatsian protagonists, is dramatized as tense ambivalence; a metamorphosis of being is necessary to resolve it. The linguistic equivalent to Madeline's ambivalence in these stanzas, of course, is the ironic interplay of religious and erotic diction; this, too, will be resolved at the poem's climax, where the suppression of desire ceases to be an issue, and the language of theology becomes the most appropriate expression of the intensity of life felt upon the pulses.

Porphyro dashes into the poem rather like the "argent revelry" that "burst" into the castle banquet hall. The revelers may be his foes, but he too is an amorous cavalier, come from across the moors "with heart on fire / For Madeline" (75-76). In obvious contrast to Madeline "Hoodwink'd with fairy fancy" (70), he displays no ambivalence at all toward what he so robustly desires:

> Beside the portal doors,
> Buttress'd from moonlight, stands he, and implores
> All saints to give him sight of Madeline,
> But for one moment in the tedious hours,

That he might gaze and worship all unseen;
Perchance speak, kneel, touch, kiss—in sooth such things have
    been.

(76-81)

Again, the narrator's tone is crucial. The melodramatic humor of
Porphyro's lurking in the shadows keeps us from seeing him as
villainous; and the eager progression of verbs from "gaze and worship" to "speak, kneel, touch, kiss" delightfully expresses Porphyro's urgent wish to propel anticipated desire into action, all this
leading to the comic truism that crowns the stanza.[12] In sooth such
things have been, and will be for him, despite all obstacles. In
short, Porphyro is not a rake. Rather, he is a healthy young man
who has endured too many solitary "tedious hours" and has
crossed the moors to follow the advice Keats once gave to his hap-
pily engaged friend Reynolds: "Gorge the honey of life" (I, 370).
    Porphyro's very amusing encounter with old Angela sustains our
impression that he personifies the poem's positive values. Against a
background of threatening "barbarian hordes, / Hyena foremen,
and hot-blooded lords, / Whose very dogs would execrations howl
/ Against his lineage" (85-88), the palsied, muttering crone tries
her senile best to protect him and eventually ministers to his every
wish. Yet despite his threats and cajoling, Porphyro does not really
exploit Angela. He knows that her prayers for him " 'each morn
and evening, / Were never miss'd' " (157-58), and she is so "weak
in body and in soul" (90) as to render any opposition to his intent
ludicrous, which is of course the underlying comic premise of the
scene. The same is true of her frenzied protectiveness toward
Madeline when Porphyro porposes his stratagem: " 'A cruel man
and impious thou art: / Sweet lady, let her pray, and sleep, and
dream / Alone with her good angels, far apart / From wicked men
like thee' " (140-43). That is, Angela's puritanical defense of
Madeline's dreaming further indicts it, and this is confirmed by
the ease with which Porphyro is able to sweep her fears aside:

Thus plaining, doth she bring
    A gentler speech from burning Porphyro;
So woful, and of such deep sorrowing,

> That Angela gives promise she will do
> Whatever he shall wish, betide her weal or woe.
>   (158-62)

For despite the blandishment in his various appeals to this "churchyard thing, / Whose passing-bell may ere the midnight toll," he is honest when he says " 'I will not harm her, by all saints I swear' "; " 'O may I ne'er find grace / When my weak voice shall whisper its last prayer, / If one of her soft ringlets I displace, / Or look with ruffian passion in her face' " (155-56, 145-49). His stratagem is indeed erotic, coming "like a full-blown rose, / Flushing his brow, and in his pained heart / Made purple riot" (136-38); but the ultimate expression of his passion is not at all "ruffian."

Porphyro conceives his stratagem in "a little moonlight room, / Pale, lattic'd, chill, and silent as a tomb" (112-13); now Angela leads him to its fulfillment in "The maiden's chamber, silken, hush'd, and chaste" (187). The justly famous stanzas depicting the chamber's intricately colored casements and the exotic delicacies Porphyro lays before his love, "Filling the chilly room with perfume light" (275), are not merely decorative; rather, they further the poem's dramatic movement from rituals involving self-deprivation and abuse of the senses to ones celebrating the sensuous and the sensual for the genuine, vitalizing pleasures they provide. And simultaneous with this gradual warming of Madeline's "chilly nest" (235) is an enhancement of what we may call the poem's spiritual ambience. This emerges through a striking transformation in Porphyro's attitude toward Madeline, which is almost always overlooked, leading to one-sided judgments of him as a manipulator and opportunist. But Porphyro ceases merely to burn once he enters Madeline's chamber. Indeed, the narrator's pointed instruction to him (and us) in stanza XXII—"Now prepare, / Young Porphyro, for gazing on that bed; / She comes, she comes again, like ring-dove fray'd and fled" (196-98)—functions like a change of key or mode in music: the melody may remain essentially the same, but its harmonies will be modulated:

> Full on this casement shone the wintry moon,
> And threw warm gules on Madeline's fair breast,

As down she knelt for heaven's grace and boon;
Rose-bloom fell on her hands, together prest,
And on her silver cross soft amethyst,
And on her hair a glory, like a saint:
She seem'd a splendid angel, newly drest,
Save wings, for Heaven:—Porphyro grew faint:
She knelt, so pure a thing, so free from mortal taint.
(217-25)

Interestingly, Keats had first written "too pure a thing, too free from mortal taint." [13] But the main point is that now Porphyro's lustfulness begins to be both tempered and enriched by what must be termed his reverence for Madeline's beauty. He continues to watch, spellbound, as she undresses and slips into bed:

Stol'n to this paradise, and so entranced,
Porphyro gazed upon her empty dress,
And listen'd to her breathing, if it chanced
To wake into a slumberous tenderness;
Which when he heard, that minute did he bless,
And breath'd himself: then from the closet crept,
Noiseless as fear in a wide wilderness,
And over the hush'd carpet, silent, stept,
And 'tween the curtains peep'd, where, lo!—how fast she slept.
(244-52)

The state of mind Keats is depicting here is of the utmost poised delicacy. It is that of the lover nearly overwhelmed by the prospect of satisfying his desire, and at the same time almost disbelieving, yet filled with gratitude, that such delight may be had. This is, indeed, a primary version of the Keatsian "paradise," [14] a rarefied blend of yearning and awe, its quiet intensity hitherto unexplored by Porphyro (hence "wide wilderness") and therefore somewhat fearful. The metamorphosis of "burning" Porphyro has begun.

The subject of his reverence is also being prepared for a transformation. Earlier, when Angela told Porphyro of "His lady's purpose," "he scarce could brook / Tears, at the thought of those enchantments cold, / And Madeline asleep in lap of legends old"

(133-35); and the dénouement of the tale proves the justness of his anxiety by dissolving such enchantment. Porphyro's regret also underlies the stanzas in which the narrator describes Madeline's preparation for sleep and her performance of the prescribed rites. Previously derided as a harmless whim, the ritual is now exposed as a serious evasion of human process, of vitality itself:

> Out went the taper as she hurried in;
> Its little smoke, in pallied moonshine, died:
> She clos'd the door, she panted, all akin
> To spirits of the air, and visions wide:
> No uttered syllable, or, woe betide!
> But to her heart, her heart was voluble,
> Paining with eloquence her balmy side;
> As though a tongueless nightingale should swell
> Her throat in vain, and die, heart-stifled, in her dell.
>
> (199-207)

The extinguished taper is the reverse of the fire and star images expressive of Porphyro's sexual exuberance throughout the poem. Similarly, the closed door hints at self-deprivation, and the grim simile of the nightingale ironically undercuts the throbbing eloquence of Madeline's anticipated fulfillment in the world of dreams.[15] Indeed, the opening and closing images indicate that her evasion is analogous to death itself (here are the seeds of the "Ode to a Nightingale").

Stanza XXVII is similarly ominous:

> Soon, trembling in her soft and chilly nest,
> In sort of wakeful swoon, perplex'd she lay,
> Until the poppied warmth of sleep oppress'd
> Her soothed limbs, and soul fatigued away;
> Flown, like a thought, until the morrow-day;
> Blissfully haven'd both from joy and pain;
> Clasp'd like a missal where swart Paynims pray;
> Blinded alike from sunshine and from rain,
> As though a rose should shut, and be a bud again.
>
> (235-43)

The kind of sleep Madeline falls into has the oppressiveness of a drug-induced trance. She retreats to a monotonous realm (note the tiresomely repetitive past participles) where sensory awareness has ceased, and this is explicitly unnatural: "As though a rose should shut, and be a bud again" (whereas Porphyro's vigorous stratagem came "Sudden . . . like a full-blown rose"). The simile denotes a reverse-transformation of precisely the sort that Madeline should not—and in the event does not—undergo. At this point we may note that Madeline's experience so far conforms to the Keatsian metamorphosis pattern. Her discontent is the same as Porphyro's (and Endymion's)—unfulfilled sexual longing, but she seeks its resolution through a corrupt means. Indeed, the poem shows that *her* falling asleep, which elsewhere in Keats's poetry leads directly to a change of being, is as it were a false start. It is real sexual experience, not vicarious dream visions, that metamorphoses Madeline into a mature woman and sends her out of her girlhood home. Keats's variation of his usual pattern indicates the priority of his values in *The Eve of St. Agnes.* This is not to say that the poem condemns dreaming per se; rather, it rejects a certain kind of dreaming, namely, that which substitutes the disembodied pleasures of reverie for the delight which real life affords.

The narrator says that Madeline's sleep was "a midnight charm / Impossible to melt as iced stream," an overt challenge to burning Porphyro; "it seem'd he never, never could redeem—From such a stedfast spell his lady's eyes" (282-83, 286-87). Yet he does, and not by physical force but, rather, through the spiritual medium of music. Still in awe of her beauty, he tenderly bids his " 'seraph fair, awake! / Thou art my heaven, and I thine eremite,' " and plays "an ancient ditty, long since mute," whose revival revives Madeline (276-77, 291):

> Her eyes were open, but she still beheld,
> Now wide awake, the vision of her sleep:
> There was a painful change, that nigh expell'd
> The blisses of her dream so pure and deep:
> At which fair Madeline began to weep,
> And moan forth witless words with many a sigh;
> While still her gaze on Porphyro would keep;

Who knelt, with joined hands and piteous eye,
Fearing to move or speak, she look'd so dreamingly.

"Ah, Porphyro!" said she, "but even now
Thy voice was at sweet tremble in mine ear,
Made tuneable with every sweetest vow;
And those sad eyes were spiritual and clear:
How chang'd thou art! how pallid, chill, and drear!
Give me that voice again, my Porphyro,
Those looks immortal, those complainings dear!
Oh leave me not in this eternal woe,
For if thou diest, my love, I know not where to go."

(298-315)

There is no need to burden these lines with philosophical commentary on the opposed claims of the ideal and the real; Madeline is no metaphysician. Rather, it is their psychological verisimilitude that makes them dramatically appropriate. Circumstances have compelled Madeline into a state of transition similar to Apollo's at the climax of *Hyperion;* such a "painful change" must be fraught with doubt and contradictory impulses. She is understandably reluctant to abandon her blissful, dissolving dream; yet, significantly, "still her gaze on Porphyro would keep." Madeline's contradictory state—wide awake, yet beholding the dream-image— prevents her from understanding why Porphyro's eyes seem sad and his aspect blanched, but the narrator makes clear the dramatic propriety of his appearance. He is so touched by her beauty that he pales at the thought of disturbing it and therefore gazes upon her with "piteous eyes, / Fearing to move or speak." Alarmed by his silence and misinterpreting his fearful look, Madeline thinks either that her deformed dream-vision will dissolve completely, or that the real Porphyro is about to die; indeed, given her confused state, it is most likely that both thoughts occur simultaneously. In any case, it is the fear of loss—not a preference for the ideal Porphyro over the real one—that makes her cry, " 'Give me that voice again, my Porphyro, / Those looks immortal, those complainings dear! / Oh *leave me not* in this eternal woe, / For if thou diest, my love, I know not where to go.' "

It is this fear that Porphyro must now assuage.

Beyond a mortal man impassion'd far
At these voluptuous accents, he arose,
Ethereal, flush'd, and like a throbbing star
Seen mid the sapphire heaven's deep repose;
Into her dream he melted, as the rose
Blendeth its odour with the violet,—
Solution sweet: meantime the frost-wind blows
Like Love's alarum pattering the sharp sleet
Against the window-panes; St. Agnes' moon hath set.
                                    (316-24)

The ritual of lovemaking incorporates, inevitably, the poem's principal dramatic motifs. The Beadsman's ascetic religiosity, echoed in Madeline's observance, has been eroticized; the revelers' hedonism, individualized in Porphyro's pursuit, has been spiritualized. Consistent with the careful development of his character, Porphyro is both ethereal and flushed, and these epithets determine the subsequent images of the throbbing star and the blended scents of violet and rose. This is indeed love poetry in the tradition of the Song of Solomon, "as purely sensuous and passionate . . . and as much an allegory of spiritual awakening," as Bernard Blackstone has justly written.[16] It is not, of course, comprehensive; Keats is also the poet of "La Belle Dame Sans Merci" and *Lamia,* and even here the frost-wind already threatens. But such a consummation was imaginatively real for Keats at this confident, relatively untroubled time in his life. Its partial truth is enduring, and is not at all undermined by what follows.

In *The Eve of St. Agnes* the act of love constitutes the lapse of ordinary consciousness common to all Keatsian metamorphoses. For Madeline, sexual initiation is obviously transforming; for Porphyro, his lovemaking is the ultimate expression of a passionate nature whose spiritual enhancement constitutes, as we have seen, an important aspect of the poem's drama. And the customary postmetamorphic movement upward and outward is also present here. Porphyro rises like a throbbing star, he urges Madeline to " 'Arise—arise! the morning is at hand' " (345), and the two lovers then flee the castle for whatever fate awaits them beyond its walls.

The stanza in which Porphyro now declares his love for Madeline has sometimes been regarded as insincere, a throwback to his blandishment of Angela, but such an interpretation mistakes its tone:

> "My Madeline! sweet dreamer! lovely bride!
> Say, may I be for aye thy vassal blest?
> Thy beauty's shield, heart-shap'd and vermeil dyed?
> Ah, silver shrine, here will I take my rest
> After so many hours of toil and quest,
> A famish'd pilgrim,—saved by miracle.
> Though I have found, I will not rob thy nest
> Saving of thy sweet self; if thou think'st well,
>   To trust, fair Madeline, to no rude infidel.
>
> (334-42)

Of course, Porphyro's toil and quest have been (this evening) quite brief, and there has been no miracle. But his religious language is primarily a continuation of his reverence for Madeline, and its deliberate exaggeration is comic, a joyful expression of achieved delight.[17] In addition, it reinforces the secular vows of the preceding lines. The stanza echoes *Romeo and Juliet* throughout, and nothing in the poem contradicts Porphyro's declaration that he is "no rude infidel."

Porphyro twice addresses Madeline as his "bride" and pledges to protect her: " 'For o'er the souther moors I have a home for thee' " (326, 334, 351); and despite lingering fears, she can no longer protest, " 'for my heart is lost in thine' " (331). The icy storm they must now face is perhaps too obvious a symbol for the threats of the adult world, but it has a certain dramatic aptness. It is the actual equivalent to the potential dangers posed by Porphyro's enemies within the castle. These the lovers seem almost magically to pass by—"They glide, like phantoms, into the wide hall"—as if the charm of love itself were ushering them out: "By one, and one, the bolts full easy slide:— / The chains lie silent on the footworn stones;— / The key turns, and the door upon its hinges groans" (361, 367-69). The implication is that the external threat will be similarly surmounted.

> And they are gone: ay, ages long ago
> These lovers fled away into the storm.

That night the Baron dreamt of many a woe,
And all his warrior-guests, with shade and form
Of witch, and demon, and large coffin-worm,
Were long be-nightmar'd. Angela the old
Died palsy-twitch'd, with meagre face deform;
The Beadsman, after thousand aves told,
For aye unsought for slept among his ashes cold.

(370-78)

As in virtually all of Keats's significant works, death is close at hand, but in *The Eve of St. Agnes* it has been deflected onto the poem's secondary characters and leaves the protagonists themselves untouched. That is, the grotesquerie with which Keats rounds out the poem makes the central erotic adventure all the more precious and joyful; in the midst of other woe, the lovers have achieved the beauty and truth they sought. The lesson is that those who experience the healthful, transforming effect of love have a chance to thrive; the merely religious or the merely hedonistic are afflicted with darker fates. The poem dramatizes the triumph of life, whose essence is love.

Notes

1. Sperry, *Keats the Poet,* p. 199.
2. A representative nineteenth-century judgment of the peom is Colvin's: "Its personages appeal to us, not so much humanly and in themselves, as by the circumstances, scenery and atmosphere admidst which we see them move. Herein lies the strength, and also the weakness, of modern romance,—its strength, inasmuch as the charm of the mediaeval colour and mystery is unfailing for those who feel it at all,—its weakness, inasmuch as under the influence of that charm both writer and reader are too apt to forget the need for human and moral truth: and without these no great literature can exist" (Sidney Colvin, *Keats* [London, 1887; reprinted London: Macmillan and Co. Ltd., 1957], p. 160). The modern reaction came first in Earl Wasserman's *The Finer Tone: Keats's Major Poems* (Baltimore; Johns Hopkins Press, 1953), pp. 97-137. Basing his analysis on selected passages in the letters, namely Keats's analogies between the workings of the imagination and Adam's dream, and human life and the "Mansion of Many Apartments," Wasserman creates a metaphysics for Keats that distorts both his poetry and the statements on which it is supposedly based. Jack Stillinger, in "The Hoodwinking of

Madeline: Scepticism in 'The Eve of St. Agnes,' *Studies in Philology* 58 (1961): 533-55, admirably pointed out the errors in Wasserman's approach, only to advance a theory of Porphyro as the consummate rake, which strikes this reader, despite Stillinger's admitted exaggeration, as both too moralistic and at odds with the poem's tone. Further, I disagree with Stillinger's contention that Madeline's self-deception is the poem's main concern, symbolizing Keats's disillusionment with the imagination. As I argue, that idea may be touched upon, but it is not the poem's focus. The most recent significant discussion of the poem is Stuart Sperry's "Romance as Wish-Fulfillment" (in *Keats the Poet,* pp. 198-220), which modifes and expands Stillinger's view of the poem as a critique of the imagination. Sperry maintains that *"St. Agnes* is a poem about the etherealizing power of human desire and passion, a further attempt at the 'material sublime.' However the particular genius of the work lies in its comprehension of the kinds of evasiveness and disguise the imagination necessarily employs in accomplishing its transformation, an awareness of the poetic process as an act of sublimation" in its modern psychological sense. He believes that *"St. Agnes* is not primarily a glorification of sexual experience or even, for all the condensed richness of its imagery, of the human senses. It is, rather, an exceptionally subtle study of the psychology of the imagination and its processes, a further testing, pursued more seriously in some of the poet's later verse, of the quality and limits of poetic belief. More than anything else, perhaps, the element most central to the poem is its concern with wish-fulfillment . . ." (p. 202). Sperry argues his case very skillfully, and there is much in it that one can assent to; but we disagree on what is of primary concern in the poem.

3. Bate, *John Keats,* p. 438.

4. Ibid., p. 446. Bate maintains critical tact with the sensible comment that "we strain at the poem when we assume that, because of Keats's more serious use of [the ideal/ real dichotomy] elsewhere, it carries an equally heavy symbolic weight at all times."

5. See James D. Boulger, "Keats' Symbolism," *ELH,* 28 (1961): 244-59, a superbly argued essay, but one that glosses over the differences in degree of ambitiousness among the poems discussed (and ignores their chronology).

6. Ward, *John Keats: The Making of a Poet,* pp. 244-245.

7. See Sperry, *Keats the Poet,* pp. 200-201, and Bate, *John Keats,* p. 440, on counterromance tendencies in the poem.

8. Stillinger, *The Poems of John Keats,* p. 300.

9. For a concise summary of the poem's myriad contrasts, see Bate, *John Keats,* p. 442.

10. The revelers' frivolity was more blatant in Keats's first draft: "Ah what are they? the idle pulse scarce stirs, / The muse should never make the spirits gay, / Away, bright dulness, laughing fools away,—" (Stillinger, *The Poems of John Keats,* p. 300).

11. The erotic sublimation involved in Madeline's credulity is unmistakable:

> They told her how, upon St. Agnes' Eve,
> Young virgins might have visions of delight,
> And soft adorings from their loves receive
> Upon the honey'd middle of the night,
> If ceremonies due they did aright;
>
> (46-50)

12. It is hard not to believe there is something autobiographical in this. Keats chooses to focus upon the comedy inherent in desire because he knows that our recognition of it can go far in assuaging the subtle self-contempt we often feel at the involuntary pull of sexuality.

13. Stillinger, *The Poems of John Keats,* p. 309.

14. M. Allott notes that "paradise" is "frequently used in both eastern and 'Gothick' tales when describing the delights of passionate love. Mrs Radcliffe has *The Italian* (1797) i chap ii, 'From this moment Vivaldi seemed to have arisen into a new existence; the whole world to him was Paradise' (1826 edn 34)" *(Keats: The Complete Poems,* p. 469).

15. The phrase "tongueless nightingale" suggests the Philomela legend, but it can only apply ironically here, since Madeline's muteness is self-imposed, and her subsequent sexual union with Porphyro is hardly depicted as rape.

16. Bernard Blackstone, *The Consecrated Urn* (London: Longmans, 1959), p. 287.

17. It may be, as Bate claims, that in this stanza Porphyro "instinctively capitalizes on her desire for the continuation of the magic of St. Agnes's Eve" *(John Keats,* p. 447), but this is at best a secondary motive.

5.

"Ode to a Nightingale": Shadows Numberless

Though a quarrel in the streets is a thing to be hated, the energies displayed in it are fine; the commonest Man shows a grace in his quarrel—By a superior being our reasonings may take the same tone—though erroneous they may be fine—This is the very thing in which consists poetry; and if so it is not so fine a thing as philosophy—For the same reason that an eagle is not so fine a thing as a truth.

Letter to George and Georgiana Keats, 19 March 1819

The most interesting question that can come before us is, How far by the persevering endeavours of a seldom appearing Socrates Mankind may be made happy—I can imagine such happiness carried to an extreme—but what must it end in?—Death—and who could in such a case bear with death—the whole troubles of life which are now frittered away in a series of years, would then be accumulated for the last days of a being who instead of hailing its approach, would leave this world as Eve left Paradise—But in truth I do not at all believe in this sort of perfectibility—the nature of the world will not admit of it—the inhabitants of the world will correspond to itself—Let the fish philosophise the ice away from the Rivers in winter time and they shall be at continual play in the tepid delight of summer. Look at the Poles and at the sands of Africa, Whirlpools and volcanoes—Let men exterminate them and I will say that they may arrive at earthly Happiness—The point at which Man may arrive is as far as the parallel state in inanimate nature and no further.

Letter to George and Georgiana Keats, 21 April 1819

I wish for death every day and night to deliver me from these pains, and then I wish death away, for death would destroy even those pains which are better than nothing. Land and Sea, weakness and decline are great separators, but death is the great divorcer for ever.

Letter to Charles Brown, 30 September 1820

Though all of Keats's great odes of 1819 are centered upon the idea of mutability, it is the "Ode to a Nightingale" whose structure is most clearly determined by the metamorphosis pattern; indeed, the ode may be considered the most telling manifestation of it in all of Keats's poetry. The precise order of the odes' composition is of course unknown, but there is some agreement that the "Nightingale" ode followed the "Ode to Psyche," which we do know was written first.[1] My feeling is that after having experimented with stanzaic structure and having announced the kind of poetry he now felt compelled to write in the "Ode to Psyche," Keats instinctively reverted to the metamorphosis pattern in the "Nightingale" ode in order to voice initially the aesthetic and moral issues that the subsequent odes take up in a somewhat more refined and abstract way. Certainly the "Nightingale" ode is the most overtly dramatic and rhetorically indeterminate of these poems (its ending is interrogative, not, like the others, declarative). It has the energy of a first attempt, and Bate's speculation—that "it was probably in the actual process of writing the 'Ode to a Nightingale' that the full possibilities of the new form at last disclosed themselves"—seems just.[2]

In every way, death stands at the center of the poem. A profound desire to die was, as Helen Vendler has finely argued, the ode's "psychological beginning";[3] and while this desire is made explicit in the imaginatively central sixth stanza, it radiates, so to speak, with gradually diminishing intensity toward both start and finish, determining the selection of details throughout. One indication of the intensity of Keats's preoccupation with death in this poem is that it appears in two modes, which we might call "painful death" and "easeful death."[4] The first is indicated in stanza III as the sad terminus of life that afflicts youth and age indiscriminately, the culmination of "The weariness, the fever, and the fret" that must be endured. Such suffering unto death is rendered largely in physiological terms ("Where palsy shakes a few, sad, last gray hairs, / Where youth grows pale, and spectre-thin, and dies") and is, as it were, rational; for despite the private reference to his dead brother Tom, the stanza mournfully insists that painful death is universally recognized: "Here, where men sit and hear each other groan." Beauty fades, new love loses the object of its desire; all is mutability. But however much regretted, painful death is at least readily comprehended. Easeful death, on the other hand, is far more private and irrational, because it involves a mysterious attractiveness. Keats's desideratum, "To cease upon the midnight with no pain," is not, as Vendler rightly notes, self-consciously suicidal; rather, it "implies a *happy* coincidence of the desire for death and a natural death itself. . . ."[5] It seems close to what Freud meant by *thanatos* and is not at all incompatible with a strong commitment to life—this, in part, is what makes it so mysterious. Easeful death is regarded as an intensity, perhaps as *the* intensity, of life; "death is life's high meed," as Keats observed in "Why did I laugh tonight" (though here the poet's nihilism seems merely self-indulgent; the sonnet records a morbid mood, whereas the ode subsumes and evaluates that mood). Clearly Keats is burdened by both kinds of death, but easeful death has the stronger claim on his imagination, since it is a subconscious impulse he can neither fully explain nor deny.[6]

The deepening sense of what death may signify largely determines the ode's dramatic development. It is a kind of metaphysical undersong to the pouring forth of the nightingale's voice, which serves as the poem's occasion, as distinguished from its raison d'être. For critical purposes, however, it is best to follow Keats's cognitive involvement with the sensuous, immediate song and to observe how and why it becomes abstracted into a symbol of ever increasing remoteness from human affairs. For, as many critics have observed, the nightingale's song represents different values at different times; but we feel this fluid and complex symbolic development to be accomplished without strain, in part because of our natural apprehension that a bird's singing contains variations in pitch, rhythm, and dynamics and is, of course, articulated temporarily. Hence its appropriateness to a poem that chronicles a succession of moods and elucidates a process of self-discovery.

The state of discontent, which always initiates the Keatsian metamorphosis pattern, is announced at once:

I

My heart aches, and a drowsy numbness pains
　My sense, as though of hemlock I had drunk,
Or emptied some dull opiate to the drains
　One minute past, and Lethe-wards had sunk:
'Tis not through envy of thy happy lot,
　But being too happy in thine happiness,—
　　That thou, light-winged Dryad of the trees,
　　　In some melodious plot
Of beechen green, and shadows numberless,
　　Singest of summer in full-throated ease.

In trying to understand the nature of Keats's discontent, we realize that this is the most ambiguous stanza of the ode. The sharp rhythmic contrast of the first line's phrases prefigures apparent contradictions in meaning; indeed, the first line is itself contradictory. The abrupt staccato beats of "My heart aches" give way to the drawn-out torpor (prolonged by the enjambment) of "a drowsy numbness pains / My sense." Somehow numbness pains, coexisting with heartache. The similes stress the narcotic aspect of Keats's reaction, but the drugs are deprived of any power to soothe; yet the poet declares he is happy—"too happy" in fact—which state, in its intensity, brings us back to pain. There is the added difficulty that, looking ahead to stanza III, Keats is indeed envious of the nightingale's happy lot. Possibly, the pain of extreme happiness can be explained by the luxuriously morbid trance and its momentous dissolution Keats experiences in stanza VI, but the emotion would seem to depend upon his having merely heard the nightingale's song without yet having probed its implications.

The sensory and emotional confusions of stanza I, however much they may submit to partial resolutions, are purposeful. They signify the extraordinary psychological disturbance the bird's singing has aroused in Keats and provide a powerful motive for his subsequent mental pursuit. For despite the airiness of the dryad image and the aptly rich and soaring last line (whose rhythm and final open vowel give it the broad effect of a hexameter), the pursuit is going to be tortuous. Keats does not know exactly where the bird is, only that it sings "In *some* melodious plot" amid "shadows numberless." This lightly sketched vagueness, linked with the previous references to opiates and the attendant logical confusions, indicates what Cleanth Brooks has called the "process of dissolution" that Keats dramatizes in the ode, a process "suggested by the imagined movement away from the world of clear outlines and sharply drawn distinctions into a world of shadows and darkness." [7] This process of dissolution can, with greater precision perhaps, be termed metamorphosis; the ode's first stanza describes one aspect of the discontent that initiates change.

The natural fullness of the nightingale's song, which Keats instinctively associates with the ancient world, leads to a desire for his own fruitful satiety in a Mediterranean paradise:

II

O, for a draught of vintage! that hath been
   Cool'd a long age in the deep-delved earth,
Tasting of Flora and the country green,
   Dance, and Provençal song, and sunburnt mirth!
O, for a beaker full of the warm South,
   Full of the true, the blushful Hippocrene,
     With beaded bubbles winking at the brim,
       And purple-stained mouth,
  That I might drink, and leave the world unseen,
    And with thee fade away into the forest dim:

By trying to imitate the bird's felicity on his own terms, Keats is making his first gesture toward comprehension and, ultimately, union. The topographical movement is inward and downward: "deep-delved earth," from Provençe to the Grecian fount; hence intoxication appears as a pleasurable falling from the clear margin of consciousness toward some vaguely apprehended center. Wine, of course, is the cheering natural counterpart to the oppressive, potentially deadly depressants of stanza I. It is thought to be an appropriate means for reaching the bird because its enlivening effect corresponds to the rich, stimulating plenitude of the nightingale's singing. But the amoral playfulness of winking bubbles and "purple-stained mouth" is short-lived; wine's power to transport inevitably reminds Keats of the world he wishes to leave "unseen" (the epithet is part of the ode's devaluation of eyesight—that is, of ordinary awareness, an idea developed fully in stanza V).

III

Fade far away, dissolve, and quite forget
  What thou among the leaves hast never known,
The weariness, the fever, and the fret
  Here, where men sit and hear each other groan;
Where palsy shakes a few, sad, last gray hairs,
  Where youth grows pale, and spectre-thin, and dies;
    Where but to think is to be full of sorrow
      And leaden-eyed despairs,
Where Beauty cannot keep her lustrous eyes,
  Or new Love pine at them beyond to-morrow.

The flow of thought is inexorable and disruptive. Whereas the nightingale's unconscious, vitally free happiness could be simply celebrated in stanza I and analogized in stanza II to earthly human pleasures (wine, greenery, dance, folksong, "sunburnt mirth"), now it must contend with what I have called painful death. But there is really no contest. In symbolic terms, the bird has begun to soar beyond Keats's human reach. Precisely because it has "never known / The weariness, the fever, and the fret" of self-conscious humanity, the nightingale becomes emblematic of some visionary world where "the essence of pleasure is extractable and indestructible." [8] Here we begin to glimpse the ode's central irony: as Keats's longing for mystic union with the bird intensifies, the more intensely does he realize their ultimate separateness. These lines prepare us for the more radical, devastating split between the two, which occurs at the poem's climax in stanza VI. At this point, however, Keats hopes to achieve an obliviousness approximating the nightingale's realm of pure, amoral pleasure.[9] To do this, a new means of escape, more potent than wine, is required, because a new discontent, more "philosophical" in nature, has been added to the sensory disturbance recorded in stanza I. The world's woe calls forth the world's balm, namely, the imagination:

IV

Away! away! for I will fly to thee,
   Not charioted by Bacchus and his pards,
But on the viewless wings of Poesy,
   Though the dull brain perplexes and retards:
Already with thee! tender is the night,
   And haply the Queen-Moon is on her throne,
     Cluster'd around by all her starry Fays;
      But here there is no light,
   Save what from heaven is with the breezes blown
     Through verdurous glooms and winding mossy ways.

V

I cannot see what flowers are at my feet,
   Nor what soft incense hangs upon the boughs,
But, in embalmed darkness, guess each sweet
   Wherewith the seasonable month endows
The grass, the thicket, and the fruit-tree wild;
   White hawthorn, and the pastoral eglantine;
     Fast-fading violets cover'd up in leaves;
      And mid-May's eldest child,
   The coming musk-rose, full of dewy wine,
     The murmurous haunt of flies on summer eves.

Incantation ("Away! away!") counters—and surmounts—the dull brain's leaden assessment of human misery; the conscious, rational faculties are greatly diminished, if not entirely suspended, and

Keats enters into an imaginative trance, imaged as a penetration of the bird's melodious plot. The nightworld that he and the nightingale share is, significantly, "tender"—that is, not oppressively, frighteningly dark. Indeed, even though the moon and stars are not visible, some light does penetrate this most luxurious bower. Such an ambience is by now familiar: the sick lovers in "I stood tip-toe" were transformed to health in their latticed chamber at evening (though a "bright and clear" one [215] to prefigure the happy eventuality); Endymion is first visited by his goddess in a shady nook during Apollo's "most kingly hour"—when "his chariot last / Its beams against the zodiac-lion cast" (I, 549, 552-53), and the mortal shepherd is apotheosized at evening in a "gloomy wood" alleviated by the suddenly revealed brightness of Cynthia (IV, 1003, 982ff.); the Apollo of *Hyperion* is metamorphosed to full divinity "in the morning twilight" (III, 33); the transforming union of Madeline and Porphyro occurs nocturnally in a room whose darkness is made tender by "pallid moonshine" (200).

What does Keats's being "with" the bird signify? If we view the ode primarily as aesthetic commentary, then clearly his trance dramatizes the power of art to transport us from mundane awareness to a finer, visionary realm where the antiphonal strains of existence are harmonized, an intense state of awareness in which all disagreeables (i.e., incompatibilities) "evaporate" and a unity of being is achieved.[10] But to speak in this way implies an even wider significance. Stanza V describes a deeply attractive pastoral utopia, with no quarrels in no streets, a serene, eternal world of natural fulfillment and utter freedom, where intuition (as opposed to awareness through the partial, categorizing senses) is perfectly comprehensive. Interestingly, this emblem of ideality is not static, for as Perkins and others have noted, "The violets are 'fast-fading,' and are being replaced by the 'coming musk-rose,' and as the poet, conscious of the process, thinks of the musk-rose, his imagination leaps ahead to the time of fulfillment and completion when the musk-rose will be 'the murmurous haunt of flies on summer eves.'"[11] In short, Keats's being "with" the nightingale signifies humanity's desire to achieve a transcendent new life of plenitude and delight, "uninfected by knowledge of sickness and death," whose scope is in the largest sense moral.[12]

But Keats does not merely depict such a realm; in the fullness of his submission to its allure, he is inexorably led to judge it:

VI

Darkling I listen; and, for many a time
  I have been half in love with easeful Death,
Call'd him soft names in many a mused rhyme,
  To take into the air my quiet breath;
Now more than ever seems it rich to die,
  To cease upon the midnight with no pain,
    While thou art pouring forth thy soul abroad
      In such an ecstasy!
Still wouldst thou sing, and I have ears in vain—
  To thy high requiem become a sod.

In these beautiful and moving lines, the ode makes its essential turn. It is a stanza of verbal dramas, which become clarified when we grasp its structure. As I read the stanza, there is one break after the quatrain and another after the foreshortened eighth line. There is a marked verbal contrast between the quatrain and the next four lines, for whereas the former is filled with unspecific, hovering phrases ("many a time," "half in love," "soft names," "many a mused rhyme") and mild, almost timid epithets ("easeful," "soft," "quiet"), the diction of the latter is precise and of high emotional intensity: "rich," "cease," "midnight," "no pain," "ecstasy." This contrast produces a crescendo effect, which crests in the foreshortened line at the word "ecstasy," whose falling rhythm evokes a profound sense of *longing*. For the ode's thematic drama, however, the stanza's more significant break is the one that is caused by this crescendo; that is, between the final two lines and everything that comes before.

The luxurious placidity of the imaginative bower that Keats shares with the nightingale prompts the poet to contemplate a more profound ease; as if his tranced union with the bird were itself a dull opiate or hemlock, he drifts toward the point of no return. This involution, of course, has been rather elaborately prepared for by images of burial from the very start: sinking "Lethe-wards," dissolving into the bird's plot of "shadows numberless,"

relishing wine "Cool'd a long age in the deep-delved earth," luxuriating in "embalmed darkness" where he guesses at "Fast-fading
violets cover'd up in leaves." In stanza VI, the nightingale's symbolic meaning shifts once again. No longer signifying simply a
pleasurable visionary realm, the bird's singing now suggests a form
of eternality involving the dissolution of life in any recognizable
mode, the transition to which Keats imagines to be voluptuous.
Indeed, his language makes it unmistakably clear that he is thinking of the moment of sexual climax—but devoid of its preceding
frenzy and infinitely prolonged. This is eternality with a vengeance.

Seduced by his imagination and urged onward by limitless desire to intensify his mystic union with the bird, Keats draws an
analogy between the nightingale's self-actualizing and what he
feels should be his own; that is, he implores the bird "To take into
the air my quiet breath . . . / While thou art pouring forth thy soul
abroad / In such an ecstasy!" Irrationally *more* than half in love
with easeful death, Keats momentarily embraces darkness; then, in
a masterstroke of irony, the mood is destroyed. For the poet's supreme imitation of the bird entails an awareness of Time: he
would become spiritually deadened *"While* thou *art pouring* forth
thy soul abroad . . ."* The bell of Time "tolls," and in a shock of
rational understanding, Keats's identification with the bird is shattered at its highest pitch. Suddenly the fatal analogy is seen for the
deception it is:

> *Still* wouldst thou sing, and I have ears in vain—
> To thy high requiem *become* a sod.

As Keats immediately laments in stanza VII, the bird's song is
changeless throughout the ages and therefore may be said to live
eternally; but he is mortal and belongs to the world of becoming.
The unconscious, purely instinctive nightingale (and others like it),
in constantly pouring forth its soul, thereby perpetuates its identity; the poet, in giving to the air his quiet breath, must relinquish
consciousness, the sole means whereby he can know the beauty of
the bird's song at all.[13] With chilling irony, all the more compelling for its mournful dignity, Keats imagines the nightingale sing-

ing his own requiem were he really to succeed in fully joining it. He realizes, in short, that the flight from pain is an evasion of *all* that life contains; for human kind, pain and joy are inseparable, as the "Ode on Melancholy" will make clear. This sobering insight into what easeful death would really mean compels the meta-morphosis of consciousness that the "Nightingale" ode dramatizes. That is, instead of embracing easeful death, he dies into a life of new, disillusioned understanding, which the remainder of the poem now probes:

VII

Thou wast not born for death, immortal Bird!
  No hungry generations tread thee down;
The voice I hear this passing night was heard
  In ancient days by emperor and clown:
Perhaps the self-same song that found a path
    Through the sad heart of Ruth, when, sick for home,
      She stood in tears amid the alien corn;
        The same that oft-times hath
    Charm'd magic casements, opening on the foam
      Of perilous seas, in fairy lands forlorn.

VIII

Forlorn! the very word is like a bell
  To toll me back from thee to my sole self!
Adieu! the fancy cannot cheat so well
  As she is fam'd to do, deceiving elf.
Adieu! adieu! thy plaintive anthem fades
    Past the near meadows, over the still stream,
      Up the hill-side; and now 'tis buried deep
       In the next valley-glades:
    Was it a vision, or a waking dream?
      Fled is that music:—Do I wake or sleep?

Stanzas VII and VIII constitute parallel distancings of the night-ingale's song, the first primarily in time, the second in space, which symbolize Keats's unhappy alienation from all that it had come to represent (accentuated by the reiterated foreign valediction

"Adieu"). The tone of stanza VII moves from ruefulness, to poignancy, ending in plaintiveness.[14] This emotional density, combined with the temporal extension, makes us feel how strenuous Keats's experience has been, and how burdensome the knowledge he has derived from it. The receding temporal images, from the historical "emperor and clown," through the more remote biblical Ruth, to the timeless realms of legend—magical but perilous and forlorn because "men cannot live in them"[15]—give a more panoramic and therefore more doleful image of downtrodden human generations than that depicted in stanza III. This is another sign of the transformation in Keats's awareness that his experience with the nightingale has fostered.

In stanza VII, after the repeated ring of "Forlorn!" (the word does what the poetry says) and "plaintive anthem," the aural images cease, displaced by ones of spatial distancing. The rhythm accentuates it: stress falls on the prepositions "Past . . . over . . . Up. . . ." The flight upward (or outward) subsequent to almost all Keatsian metamorphoses is here ironically transferred from the protagonist, who is significantly earthbound, to the independent stimulus of his transformative meditation. The nightingale's song, once a presumed "high requiem" but here diminished to a "plaintive anthem," now "fades" into the far countryside—an ironic reminiscence of the poet's former wish to "fade far away" into the bird's melodious plot and of his subsequent spiritual estrangement. Ironic, too, is Keats's observation that it is now "buried deep / In the next valley-glades," the final twist of the burial motif, since the song cannot die. Irony, of course, is a sign of rational perspective, and the stanza confirms the poet's return to normal but renovated self-consciousness, to lonely communion with his "sole self." The tone almost shades into the sardonic at "Adieu! the fancy cannot cheat so well / As she is fam'd to do, deceiving elf"; but this judgment stops short of being bitter. For despite the poet's disillusionment, the experience has permitted him a new discrimination, not only of easeful death, but of the mind's—specifically the imagination's—natural limits: the fancy cannot cheat *so well* as she is famed to do. Keats's disillusionment, however, spreads far beyond this. It is the whole construct of ideality symbolized by the luxurious harmonization of stanza V that has become equivocal, because our exacerbated longing for it, so Keats's experience has revealed, is a concealed form of death-worship.

Yet the ode concludes not with declaration, but with questioning. Was Keats's visionary insight genuine or merely a subjective sham? When was he truly awake to reality—then or now? My feeling is that the first of these questions is answered by what can only be called the poem's true voice of feeling: the experience *was* genuinely revelatory and permanently valuable. But "Do I wake or sleep?" seems to me a false dichotomy, for both the imaginative trance and the poet's subsequent disillusionment are validly "wakeful"—that is, insightful—states, though of varying intensities and offering diverse kinds of knowledge.[16] The real point of these questions, however, may be to express the fatigue, and perhaps the humility, that Keats's listening to the nightingale has inspired. Such emotions would constitute an aesthetically decorous finale to the ode's drama and sustain the mature honesty of response that Keats has demonstrated from the opening lines onward. Indeed, given the issues it raises, one comes away from the "Ode to a Nightingale" admiring perhaps most of all the poet's courage.

As I hope my reading has made clear, the "Ode to a Nightingale" is the most complex and sophisticated expression of the Keatsian metamorphosis pattern we have so far encountered. To recapitulate briefly, the poet moves from a discontent that is both sensory and ontological, into a visionary trance in which a seductive morbidity is acknowledged but disavowed, which leads to a more deeply apprehended awareness of mortal limits. Each of the three parts of the pattern is more elaborate in this poem than is its counterpart in Keats's previous work, a sign of the poet's increasing artistic maturity. That is, the refinement of poetic technique, which critics have long recognized in the great odes of 1819, has, as it were, permitted Keats to release his deepest imaginative impulses with greater comprehensiveness and subtlety than he had heretofore done. Nowhere else is the poet's profound morbidity more frankly admitted; nowhere else is it more urgently conquered. The effort required is reflected in the welter of emotions we observed in stanzas VII and VIII and in the fatigue at the close.

Just as Madeline and Porphyro emerge from their sheltered lovemaking into the storm outside, so in the ode does Keats leave the nightingale's blissful imaginative bower to inhabit a real world of meadows and streams, hillsides and valley-glades, though the tempest he suffers is internalized. Beyond this point the analogy cannot be pressed; *The Eve of St. Agnes* is a high-spirited romance written in the flush of first love, whereas "Ode to a Nightingale" records a far more equivocal, desperate, and—it must be said— morally compelling experience. But by perceiving the same overall structural pattern underlying both, we can measure the development of Keats's imaginative powers, as well as see a significant shift in his attitude toward issues that have preoccupied him from the start of his career. David Perkins, among others, has observed that "the over-all course of [Keats's] development might be partly described as a periodic, though gradually cumulative, loss of confidence in the merely visionary imagination." [17] A survey of post-metamorphic states in Keats's work confirms this. The sick lovers in "I stood tip-toe" are cured; Adonis wakes to reunion with Venus, Glaucus is rejuvenated and the drowned lovers revived, the mortal Endymion, when all is said and done, is enskyed with his goddess, although the poem's incongruities and lack of enthusiasm at the close clearly suggest a burgeoning distrust of the visionary. But Apollo's deification is premised upon his knowing the tragedy inherent in historical progress (even the reign of divinities—the ideal world itself—is mutable), and *The Eve of St. Agnes* is rather similarly ambiguous, a romance whose conventions are hedged, even threatened, by a tougher sense of reality; hence the lovers' joyful union *and* the "elfin-storm" whose "iced gusts" nevertheless "still rave and beat," its "frost wind . . . / Like Love's alarm pattering the sharp sleet / Against the window panes." This is either exquisitely poised, or an evasion, depending on one's needs. "Ode to a Nightingale" has a different kind of poise, and evades nothing.

The prose analogue to "Ode to a Nightingale" (and somewhat less directly to "Ode on a Grecian Urn" and "Ode on Melancholy") is Keats's famous metaphor of life as a "vale of Soul-making" (II, 101-4), written just nine days before the "Ode to Psyche." Rejecting the orthodox Christian view of human existence as merely probationary, Keats posits "a grander system of salvation

than the chrystain religion—or rather it is a system of Spirit-creat-
ing," "which does not affront our reason and humanity":

> The common cognomen of this world among the misguided
> and superstitious is "a vale of tears" from which we are to be
> redeemed by a certain arbitrary interposition of God and
> taken to Heaven—What a little circumscribed straightened
> notion! Call the world if you Please "The vale of Soul-mak-
> ing" Then you will find out the use of the world (I am speak-
> ing now in the highest terms for human nature admitting it to
> be immortal which I will here take for granted for the purpose
> of showing a thought which has struck me concerning it) I say
> *"Soul making"* Soul as distinguished from an Intelligence—
> There may be intelligences or sparks of the divinity in mil-
> lions—but they are not Souls till they acquire identities, till
> each one is personally itself. Intelligences are atoms of percep-
> tion—they know and they see and they are pure, in short they
> are God—how then are Souls to be made? How then are these
> sparks which are God to have identity given them—so as ever
> to possess a bliss peculiar to each ones individual existence?
> How but by the medium of a world like this?

> Do you not see how necessary a World of Pains and troubles is
> to school an Intelligence and make it a soul? A Place where
> the heart must feel and suffer in a thousand diverse ways!

The vale of soulmaking is a more deeply meditated version of the
mansion of many apartments; bolder and more comprehensive in
scope, it constitutes Keats's theodicy. Since living is necessarily a
perpetual confrontation with "a World of Pains and troubles," it
implicitly involves constant self-renewal, which is ultimately edu-
cative and morally enriching. Whereas orthodoxy "assumed that
the soul in each individual was already created by God before it
came into this world," for Keats "there was specifically no such
precreation. God creates souls in the world, indeed, through the
trials and probations of the world." [18] To the Christian, self-trans-
formation is limited to repentance; one's essentially sinful nature is
immutable until it is "redeemed by a certain arbitrary interpo-

sition of God . . ." To Keats the humanist, metamorphoses of "sparks of the divinity" are the means whereby the soul simultaneously acquires identity and comes to know its native space of beauty and pain.

Notes

1. Of the spring odes that follow "Psyche," Bate notes that "Conventional opinion has placed the 'Ode to a Nightingale' first, in late April or early May, then the 'Grecian Urn' and 'Melancholy,' and finally the 'Ode on Indolence' " (*John Keats,* p. 498).
2. Ibid., pp. 500-501.
3. Helen Vendler, "The Experiential Beginnings of Keats's Odes," *Studies in Romanticism* 12 (1973): 593.
4. A similar distinction, applied to considerations somewhat different from my own, is made in Dorothy Van Ghent's fine essay, "The Passion of the Groves," *Sewanee Review* 52 (1944): 226-46.
5. Vendler, "The Experiential Beginnings . . . ," 593fn. (italics added).
6. Vendler claims that death in stanza III is "safely distanced" from Keats's immediate concerns by "being externalized, allegorized, and deceptively broadened . . . to include gray hairs and palsy" (594). There is, as I argue, a kind of dramatic strategy involved in the difference between painful and easeful death; therefore, I do not detect any deception in stanza III.
7. "The Artistry of Keats: A Modern Tribute," in *The Major English Romantic Poets: A Symposium in Reappraisal,* ed. C. D. Thorpe, Carlos Baker, and Bennet Weaver (Carbondale, Southern Illinois Univ. Press, 1957), p. 249.
8. James Boulger, "Keats' Symbolism," *ELH* 28 (1961): 246.
9. David Perkins comments on how stanza III builds upon the poem's opening lines: "Mortal existence, as the poet thinks of it, has a distorted and ghastly resemblance to his own state of mind in the first stanza. As he hears the nightingale's song, so 'men sit and hear each other groan.' The poet has been drowsy as though drugged; men are weary. He has been glutted or 'too happy' with the song of the nightingale; men are 'full of sorrow' " (*The Quest for Permanence* [Cambridge, Mass.: Harvard Univ. Press, 1959], p. 249).
10. Van Ghent speaks of "an actual harmonization attained, even though no feeling is stated and only sense impressions are presented—darkness, fragrance, various herbage and flowers" ("The Passion of the Groves," 245). One may note a subtle blending of religious mysticism ("incense") with sexuality ("The coming musk-rose, full of dewy wine, / The murmurous haunt of flies on summer eves"). The overall effect of the stanza is wonderfully peculiar, in part because of the pervasive synthesia, in part because the visual imagery makes us see particulars without being able to localize them in relation to one another. R. H. Fogle comments similarly: "The forest scene is

Romantically picturesque, without being really pictorial: one does not visualize it, but its composition is describable in visual metaphor. Its unity is a matter of blending, with objects softened and distanced by the veil of darkness . . ." ("Keats's Ode to a Nightingale," *PMLA* 68 [1953]: 215).

11. Perkins, *The Quest for Permanence,* p. 251.

12. Van Ghent, "The Passion of the Groves," 244.

13. To the old charge of illogicality leveled at the stanza's opening, namely that this particular nightingale, like the poet, will in fact die, the simplest and best explanation is Brooks's: "The nightingale . . . though it will die, was 'not born to die'—[it] lives without consciousness of death" ("The Artistry of Keats: A Modern Tribute," p. 250). Perkins notes that "in its distance from the poet the nightingale has now been *openly* transformed into symbol." "Here, of course, Keats employs a brilliant poetic tact to justify the symbolic assertion. By referring only to the voice of the nightingale, he can identify it with all nightingales and so find a natural basis for claiming that, like the urn, it has remained 'in midst of other woe / Than ours, a friend to man' " (*The Quest for Permanence,* p. 254; italics added).

14. Vendler points out the tacit irony that unifies the diverse tonalities of stanza VII: ". . . though Keats's bitterness and plaintiveness preclude any truce or compact between himself and the nightingale proper, he does make a compact of fellowship with the other listeners to the bird: 'The voice I hear this passing night was heard' by countless others. *There* is the true connection and link . . ." ("The Experiential Beginnings . . . ," p. 595).

15. Perkins, *The Quest for Permanence,* p. 255.

16. Different readings of the ode, of course, produce different interpretations of these questions. Among critics for whom the poem is primarily a commentary on the imagination, Harold Bloom has given perhaps the most succinct response to Keats's concluding ambivalence: "is the act and state of creation a heightening or merely an evasion of the state of experience? Once back in experience, the honest answer is only in the continued question, both as to fact and to will: 'Do I wake or sleep?' " (*The Visionary Company* [Garden City, N.Y.: Doubleday, 1961], p. 432).

17. Perkins, *The Quest for Permanence,* p. 220.

18. Robert Gittings, *John Keats* (Boston: Little, Brown, 1968), p. 308.

6.

Lamia: Perplexed Delight

I have never known any unalloy'd Happiness for many days together: the death or sickness of some one has always spoilt my hours—and now when none such troubles oppress me, it is you must confess very hard that another sort of pain should haunt me. Ask yourself my love whether you are not very cruel to have so entrammelled me, so destroyed my freedom.

          —Letter to Fanny Brawne, 1 July 1819

. . . however I should like to enjoy what the competences of life procure, I am in no wise dashed at a different prospect. I have spent too many thoughtful days & moralized thro' too many nights for that, and fruitless would they be indeed, if they did not by degrees make me look upon the affairs of the world with a healthy deliberation. I have of late been moulting: not for fresh feathers & wings: they are gone, and in their stead I hope to have a pair of patient sublunary legs. I have altered, not from a Chrysalis into a butterfly, but the Contrary, having

two little loopholes, whence I may look out into the stage of
the world.

—Letter to J. H. Reynolds, 11 July 1819

Even as I leave off—it seems to me that a few more moments
thought of you would uncrystallize and dissolve me—I must
not give way to it—but turn to my writing again—if I fail I
shall die hard—O my love, your lips are growing sweet again
to my fancy—I must forget them—

—Letter to Fanny Brawne, 16 August 1819

Keats wrote the first part of *Lamia* at Shanklin, on the Isle of
Wight, where he shared lodgings with his witty, ailing friend
James Rice. Suffering again from a sore throat, he complained to
Fanny (in the same letter accusing her of having entrammeled his
freedom) that "when the lonely day has closed, and the lonely
silent, unmusical Chamber is waiting to receive me as into a Sepul-
chre, then believe me my passion gets entirely the sway . . ." (II,
122). Later he spoke of that sepulchral chamber as his "little coffin
of a room at Shanklin . . ." (II, 141). Suppressed desire, the wittily
oppressive Rice, pain at the back of the throat, a morbidly confin-
ing room—from these pressures it is but a short step to the perverse
ambience of *Lamia.* Keats finished Part I of the poem by July 11
(II, 128); on that day he described himself to Reynolds as having
"of late been moulting." The metaphor paradoxically combines
calm (no doubt the result of having completed a significant piece
of work) with claustrophobia; that is, the self-deprecatory denial of
fresh feathers and wings for patient, sublunary legs that would
cleave steadily to the world, is subtly challenged by the figure of
the chrysalis, which suggests a potentially stifling inwardness, a
forced withdrawal. For this metamorphosis from butterfly to
chrysalis is unnatural, and is a far truer expression of Keats's mood
during the summer of 1819 than his claim to be looking upon the
affairs of the world with "a healthy deliberation." Indeed, the
chrysalis image is a benign version of his cry to Fanny that she has
so entrammeled him, so destroyed his freedom.

Keats's metaphor of unnatural moulting is an unconscious epitome of *Lamia,* a work that often strikes readers as uncharacteristic and whose critical history attests to its perplexing impact. Robert Gittings probably speaks for many when he says that "It somehow holds off and repels the reader just where it should most attract and impress. For all its power, there is something about it which puts us on our guard." [1] Though it is still sometimes claimed that the poem's undeniably disturbing effect is due to confusion on Keats's part, his inability to reconcile the issues he raises, most critics now argue that irresolution is precisely the point and signifies Keats's honesty in presenting a world in which all is ambiguity.[2] This is almost certainly true, and it is possible to account for the poem's peculiar effect by untangling its contrary attitudes toward love, the imagination, the reasoning mind, and so forth. But perhaps a more revealing approach is to examine the nature of the poem's myriad metamorphoses, for by so doing we can observe how, within the texture of the poetry itself, Keats is perverting his customary procedures and thereby producing a kind of inverted reading of his own previous work.[3]

The first indication of self-parody occurs in the poem's opening episode in which Hermes and Lamia strike a cynical bargain: she agrees to dissolve the charm of invisibility whereby she had hitherto protected a nymph, whom the "ever-smitten" Hermes is now pursuing, from "the love-glances of unlovely eyes" (I, 7, 102), in exchange for his metamorphosing her from snake to woman so that she may pursue the mortal Lycius. Since the union of Hermes and the nymph flowers into endless mutual bliss and the love of Lamia and Lycius terminates in mutual disaster, the juxtaposition of this brief prelude with the main narrative would seem to signify Keats's rather bitter belief that love can survive only as an ideal value, not in actual experience. Elsewhere in Keats's poetry this familiar contrast between mortal and immortal realms leads to other, usually less grim, conclusions; but the important point is that in his previous work some definite thematic statement is made through the contrast because the opposed worlds are appropriately characterized and clearly distinguished. Such is not the case in *Lamia.* As has often been pointed out, Hermes, though an immortal, is made to seem a travesty of the ideal, and the nymph is too insignificant a figure to stand for anything.[4] (There is the additional difficulty of accurately assessing Lamia's essential nature, which further compromises the juxtaposition.) Like a naughty truant, the god, "bent warm on amorous theft," has "stolen light, / On this side of Jove's clouds, to escape the sight / Of his great summoner" (I, 8, 9-11). His *spasimi d'amore* are merely amusing—"a celestial heat / Burnt from his winged heels to either ear"—or ludicrous: "And so he rested, on the lonely ground, / Pensive, and full of painful jealousies / Of the Wood-Gods, and even the very trees" (I, 22-23, 32-34). " 'Too frail of heart!' " Lamia exclaims to him (though she is hardly the one to utter such an accusation), and the God's oath of service to her is made to seem untrustworthy, in accordance with classical tradition: "Light flew his earnest words, among the blossoms blown" (I, 93, 91; Keats applies the suggestive epithet "light" to winged Hermes three times in the first ninety-one lines).[5] His bargaining with Lamia is less clever than self-indulgent; in short, he is lacking in either heroism, nobility, or grand passion—the qualities Keats always associates with the ideal.

Yet despite their lack of moral stature, Keats grants both Hermes and the nymph fulfillment via metamorphoses that recall those of several immortal or immortalized figures in his previous work. In part he does this in order to stress by contrast the very unnatural transformation of Lamia, which immediately follows theirs; but his deeper and much more cynical motive is to further undercut the notion of ideality by bestowing it upon inconsequential beings:

The God on half-shut feathers sank serene,
She breath'd upon his eyes, and swift was seen
Of both the guarded nymph near-smiling on the green.
It was no dream; or say a dream it was,
Real are the dreams of Gods, and smoothly pass
Their pleasures in a long immortal dream.
One warm, flush'd moment, hovering, it might seem
Dash'd by the wood-nymph's beauty, so he burn'd;
Then, lighting on the printless verdure, turn'd
To the swoon'd serpent, and with languid arm,
Delicate, put to proof the lythe Caducean charm.

So done, upon the nymph his eyes he bent
Full of adoring tears and blandishment,
And toward her stept. . . .

(I, 123-36)

The impact on Hermes of Lamia's charms, which results in something newly seen, recalls the effect of Cynthia's visitations on Endymion: the passionately impatient god swoons ("sank serene"),
then alights to return the favor and claim his dream come true—a
new life of endless erotic bliss in the "green-recessed woods" (I,
144)—reminiscent of the nightingale's melodious plot of immortal
ecstasy. The nymph, after being made visible, is then metamorphosed from a state of fearful maidenhood to one of fully realized sexuality:

she, like a moon in wane,
Faded before him, cower'd, nor could restrain
Her fearful sobs, self-folding like a flower
That faints into itself at evening hour:
But the God fostering her chilled hand,
She felt the warmth, her eyelids open'd bland,
And, like new flowers at morning song of bees,
Bloom'd, and gave up her honey to the lees.
Into the green-recessed woods they flew;
Nor grew they pale, as mortal lovers do.

(I, 136-45)

Both the nature of her change and the imagery describing it recall
Madeline's transformation: the "moon in wane" ("St. Agnes'
moon hath set"), "her chilled hand" (Madeline trembles "in her
soft and chilly nest" before experiencing Porphyro's warmth), and
especially the flower images. The nymph's anguished retreat—"self-
folding like a flower / That *faints* into itself *at evening hour*" (again
the auspicious time for change is evoked)—echoes Madeline in her
girlish avoidance of real love—"As though a rose should shut, and
be a bud again." Both females bloom into *"new* flowers" and gorge
the honey of life. And, as usual in Keatsian metamorphoses,
Hermes and the nymph soar away: "Into the green-recessed woods
they flew; / Nor grew they pale, as mortal lovers do."

Obviously, the smooth-talking god and the smooth-lipped serpent can strike their bargain because both suffer from the same love-sickness. As Hermes hovers in jealous discontent, he hears Lamia's mournful cry:

"When from this wreathed tomb shall I awake!
When move in a sweet body fit for life,
And love, and pleasure, and the ruddy strife
Of hearts and lips! Ah, miserable me!"

(I, 38-41)

Lamia's explicit wish for metamorphosis, to leave her moribund serpentine state and die into a life of erotic indulgence, seems at first unambiguous; but Keats's subsequent descriptions of her are so calculatedly enigmatic that we cannot know what such a change might signify. It is not just that she is simultaneously fascinating and grotesque, compassionate and conniving, and—most incomprehensible of all—a knowledgeable sexual novice ("A virgin purest lipp'd, yet in the lore / Of love deep learned to the red heart's core"; "As though in Cupid's college she had spent / Sweet days a lovely graduate, still unshent, / And kept his rosy terms in idle languishment" [I, 189-90, 197-99]). The real perplexity is that her original, essential state of being is unknowable. Keats deliberately teases us out of thought: "She seem'd, at once, some penanced lady elf, / Some demon's mistress, or the demon's self" (I, 55-56). Lamia pleadingly tells Hermes: " 'I was a woman, let me have once more / A woman's shape, and charming as before' " (I, 117-18). But, as Bate points out, this "does not mean she was [a woman] originally. . . . Nor do we know whether she is a mortal or an immortal, or something that falls between, or, more probably, something essentially different from either category though capable of participating in both." [6] She is, in a word, shifty, like her snakeskin:

. . . a gordian shape of dazzling hue,
Vermilion-spotted, golden, green, and blue;
Striped like a zebra, freckled like a pard,
Eyed like a peacock, and all crimson barr'd;
And full of silver moons, that, as she breathed,

Dissolv'd, or brighter shone, or interwreathed
Their lustres with the gloomier tapestries—
                                    (I, 47-53)

Because Lamia's original state is unknowable, all her metamorphoses must be viewed as changes of *appearance, not essence* (she wants a "woman's *shape,*" and later, to secure Lycius' love, she "threw the goddess off, and won his heart / More pleasantly by playing woman's part" [I, 336-37]). This is the crucial point. Elsewhere in Keats's poetry, transformations are always from one definite state to another, each of which may be assigned a clear moral value. But the figure of Lamia defies moral evaluation. Thus it is that her metamorphoses throughout the poem constitute deliberate self-parody on Keats's part, a cynical undermining of one of his deepest imaginative impulses.

In broad outline, the stages of Lamia's transformation—from a "cirque-couchant" snake-form, entombed in amorous longing, to a magically free-ranging, satisfied woman-shape—follow the familiar metamorphosis pattern. It is Keats's handling of her deathlike swoon that distinguishes it from its predecessors:

Left to herself, the serpent now began
To change; her elfin blood in madness ran,
Her mouth foam'd, and the grass, therewith besprent,
Wither'd at dew so sweet and virulent;
Her eyes in torture fix'd and anguish drear,
Hot, glaz'd, and wide, with lid-lashes all sear,
Flash'd phosphor and sharp sparks, without one cooling tear.
The colours all inflam'd throughout her train,
She writh'd about, convuls'd with scarlet pain.
A deep volcanian yellow took the place
Of all her milder-mooned body's grace;
And, as the lava ravishes the mead,
Spoilt all her silver mail, and golden brede;
Made gloom of all her frecklings, streaks and bars,
Eclips'd her crescents, and lick's up her stars,
So that, in moments few, she was undrest
Of all her sapphires, greens, and amethyst,

And rubious-argent: of all these bereft,
Nothing but pain and ugliness were left.

                                        (I, 146-64)

One need only contrast this transformation to the nymph's closing
and opening like a flower to grasp its perversity; the images drawn
from nature to describe Lamia's change suggest not fecundity but
destructive power: withered grass, the lava-ravished mead, tar-
nished metals, extinguished planets.

Still shone her crown; that vanish'd, also she
Melted and disappear'd as suddenly;
And in the air, her new voice luting soft,
Cried "Lycius! gentle Lycius!"—Borne aloft
With the bright mists about the mountains hoar
These words dissolv'd: Crete's forests heard no more.

                                        (I, 165-70)

Lamia is self-consumed by a wild metamorphic heat; such a *reductio ad nihilum* does not occur in other Keatsian transformations, and
it signals the unnaturalness of what Lamia is accomplishing.[7] Similarly, the somewhat ludicrous travail of her change makes it seem
suspect and malign. Some of the details, particularly Lamia's
being "convuls'd with scarlet pain," do recall Apollo's "pang / As
hot as death's is chill," his fiercely convulsive dying into life; but
such a comparison merely highlights the far more telling differences between the two metamorphoses.[8] Apollo's transformation is
painful because the knowledge he absorbs is that of the general
tragedy; during his supreme moment he is a kind of surrogate, a
pagan Christ enduring the misery of the world. But Lamia suffers
for herself alone, and her anguish results in no higher moral awareness. She has merely metamorphosed from one false state to
another, for though Keats says she is "now a lady bright, / A full-
born beauty new and exquisite" (I, 171-72), the lines are heavily
ironic. Lamia is not a woman; she merely looks like one. Her metamorphosis is spurious and will therefore serve to deceive, though
the falseness may be attractive and the deception sweet.

Like the song of the nightingale, Lamia's "new voice luting soft"

Lycius' name "dissolved," "Borne aloft / With the bright mists about the mountains hoar . . . ," whereupon the "full-born beauty new and exquisite" flees toward Corinth. She eventually descends, at "the moth-time of that evening dim" (I, 220), to the shore of Cenchreas, near Corinth, where she awaits the return of Lycius from the isle of Egina, the site of his sacrifice to Jove in hopes of obtaining a happy marriage.[9] "Jove heard his vows, and better'd his desire," for as Lycius wanders about, his mind wrapped in Platonic mysteries "where reason fades," he hears Lamia's plaintive command to look back; "He did; not with cold wonder fearingly, / But Orpheus-like at an Eurydice" (I, 229, 235, 247-48).[10] This deft exposition of Lycius' fatal longing leads without strain to Lamia's instantaneous enchantment of her mortal prey ("Her soft look growing coy, she saw his chain so sure" [I, 256]). With both retrospective and prophetic irony, Keats has Lycius beg Lamia not to disappear: " 'Even as thou vanishest so I shall die' " (I, 260), and when Lamia coquettishly threatens to do so, Lycius, "sick to lose / The amorous promise of her lone complain, / Swoon'd, murmuring of love, and pale with pain" (I, 287-89):

> The cruel lady, without any show
> Of sorrow for her tender favourite's woe,
> But rather, if her eyes could brighter be,
> With brighter eyes and slow amenity,
> Put her new lips to his, and gave afresh
> The life she had so tangled in her mesh:
> And as he from ne trance was wakening
> Into another, she began to sing, . . .
>
> Lycius from death awoke into amaze,
> To see her still, and singing so sweet lays;
> Then from amaze into delight he fell
> To hear her whisper woman's lore so well;
> And every word she spake entic'd him on
> To unperplex'd delight and pleasure known.
>   (I, 290-97, 322-27)

Lycius' reanimation recalls those of the sick lovers in "I stood

tip-toe," Endymion's numerous revivals, Adonis' awakening, Glaucus and the drowned lovers' rejuvenation, even the experience of
the speaker in the "Nightingale" ode (Lamia's singing is emphasized throughout this scene). But Lycius' transformation from a
state of lovelorn discontent to his new condition of unperplexed
delight is essentially false, merely the transition from one empty
trance to another: "Lycius from death awoke into amaze." Moreover, Keats stresses the speciousness of this dying into meaningless
life by having it transpire in a context of deception; that is, both
before and after it occurs, Lamia lies to Lycius about her nature,
her desires, and her previous existence. She is not one of those
" 'finer spirits' " who " 'cannot breathe below / In human climes,
and live' "; she does not want to abandon him; she is not "a
woman, and without / Any more subtle fluid in her veins / Than
throbbing blood . . ."; she has not been "so long in Corinth, where,
she said, / She dwelt but half retir'd and there had led / Days
happy as the gold coin could invent / Without the aid of love" (see
I, 271-321).

The combined effect on the reader of Lamia's unnatural metamorphosis and Lycius' specious dying into life is primarily one of
uneasiness, which seems to extend even to the characters themselves. That is, as if further to betray the falseness of their transformations, Keats concludes Part I of *Lamia* by stressing not the
lovers' joy but, rather, their enusing anxiety. Their magic flight
into Corinth is hardly triumphant: "Muffling his face, of greeting
friends in fear, / Her fingers he press'd hard . . ." (I, 362-63). They
shrink from Apollonius—" 'to-night he seems / The ghost of folly
haunting my sweet dreams' " (I, 376-77)—and vanish into a
charmed palace viewless to the nonelect. The motif of *reductio ad
nihilum* recurs both here—at the end of "Act One"—and, of course,
at the poem's conclusion.

Lamia's magical, if limited, powers and the remote, otherworldly aspect of her abode suggest that Keats intended her to
represent, at least in part, the visionary imagination. But the symbolism is made highly complex by Keats's insistence on her equivocal nature and his vacillating attitude toward her eroticism.[11] In
broad outline, however, Lamia and Lycius' sexual liaison would

seem to represent the visionary imagination's capacity simultaneously to delight and to deceive. Lamia's charms are beguiling; they
"cheat," as Keats said of the fancy in the "Nightingale" ode. What
has changed in the interval between the two poems is his attitude
toward such attractive deception—from fatigued acceptance to
cynical anger mixed with pitiful regret. This ambiguous stance is
expressed dramatically in Part II of *Lamia* by the manner in which
the lovers' passion disintegrates (and, of course, by the poem's
abrupt, fatal dénouement).

The inevitable course that Keats now thinks love must run is
announced by the two cynical maxims that open Part II:

> Love in a hut, with water and a crust,
> Is—Love, forgive us!—cinders, ashes, dust;
> Love in a palace is perhaps at last
> More grievous torment than a hermit's fast:—
> That is a doubtful tale from fairy land,
> Hard for the non-elect to understand.
>
> (II, 1-6)

But the love of Lamia and Lycius comes to grief even before it can
"breed distrust and hate, that make the soft voice hiss" (I, 10). It
begins to break down when the pressure, as it were, of its own
perfection is punctured by "a thrill / Of trumpets" from the ordinary world, which "left a thought, a buzzing in [Lycius'] head" (II,
27-29). Incapable of harboring indefinitely in "That purple-lined
palace of sweet sin" (II, 31), Lycius insists upon staging a public
marriage. In the poem's framework of ideas, this insistence represents the desire to project visionary experience into mundane reality, to effect a blending of the ideal and the real. We might expect
Keats, at this stage of his writing, to show this desire to be risky or
even impossible; unexpectedly, however, he makes such a desire
seem sadistic. Lycius tells Lamia he wants " 'to entangle, trammel
up and snare / Your soul in mine, and labyrinth you there / Like
the hid scent in an unbudded rose' " (II, 52-54). He wants to
arouse envy and submission, not love: " 'What mortal hath a prize,
that other men / May be confounded and abash'd withal, / But

lets it sometimes pace abroad majestical. . . . / Let my foes choke, and my friends shout afar . . .' " (II, 57-59, 62). Lamia, her protests unavailing, is finally reduced to masochistic surrender:

> The lady's cheek
> Trembled; she nothing said, but, pale and meek,
> Arose and knelt before him, wept a rain
> Of sorrows at his words; at last with pain
> Beseeching him, the while his hand she wrung,
> To change his purpose. He thereat was stung,
> Perverse, with stronger fancy to reclaim
> Her wild and timid nature to his aim:
> Besides, for all his love, in self despite,
> Against his better self, he took delight
> Luxurious in her sorrows, soft and new.
> His passion, cruel grown, took on a hue
> Fierce and sanguineous as 'twas possible
> In one whose brow had no dark veins to swell.
> Fine was the mitigated fury, like
> Apollo's presence when in act to strike
> The serpent—Ha, the serpent! certes, she
> Was none. She burnt, she lov'd the tyranny,
> And all subdued, consented to the hour
> When to the bridal he should lead his paramour.
>
> (II, 64-83)

This ugly and powerful scene, quite unlike anything else in Keats's poetry, constitutes an inversion of all the poet's previous love-values.[12] The contrast with *The Eve of St. Agnes* is especially telling. In both poems, the characters are altered by erotic experience, but in the earlier work Porphyro became benevolent in his eagerness and discovered the spiritual transcendence of sexual love, while Madeline was submissive for the morally valid reason of dispelling her delusions. By contrast, Lycius' manliness (such as it is) decays into brutality, while Lamia's exotic femininity is reduced to perverse tragic resignation. In *The Eve of St. Agnes* Keats portrayed sexuality as simply pleasurable partly because it signified the release from dream-life into a world of adventurous reality; whereas in *Lamia* he makes it appear cloying, a force generating distrust and hate, thereby symbolizing any state of being which, however appealing, is undermined by man's perverse compulsion to destroy the very thing that sustains him.[13]

This inversion of love-values is accompanied by a reversal of roles in the drama: whereas in Part I Lamia had been, for the most part, self-seeking, seductive, powerful, and Lycius vacuous, submissive, adoring, now in Part II he becomes the cruel victimizer and she his pathetic prey. Both the inversion of values and the reversal of roles are congruent with the unnatural and specious metamorphoses of Part I; indeed, everything in the poem involves an undermining of Keats's customary poetic procedure and beliefs. This is primarily why, as Gittings says, *Lamia* "holds off and repels the reader just where it should most attract and impress."

Following both Corinthian and Keatsian custom, the climax of Lamia's and Lycius' affair occurs "at blushing shut of day" (II, 107). Lamia, "in pale contented sort of discontent" (II, 135), prepares for her doom by magically ornamenting their banquet room, and the style of the decor, whose oddness has not been commented upon, reveals further ambiguities that sabotage our efforts to make clear moral judgments of the characters and suggest that the subsequent "wreath-passage" (in which the narrator awards symbolic crowns to the principals) is a parody of such efforts.[14] The salient characteristics of Lamia's decor are its mathematical precision and its geometricity. The mystery of its provenance is nearly conquered by its insistence on "rule and line," which is, of course, the charge made against Philosophy later on:

Fresh carved cedar, mimicking a glade
Of palm and plantain, met from either side,
High in the midst, in honour of the bride:
Two palms and then two plantains, and so on,
From either side their stems branch'd one to one
All down the aisled place; and beneath all
There ran a stream of lamps straight on from wall to wall. . . .
Between the tree-stems, marbled plain at first,

Came jasper pannels; then, anon, there burst
Forth creeping imagery of slighter trees,
And with the larger wove in small intricacies. . . .

   Of wealthy lustre was the banquet-room,
Fill'd with pervading brilliance and perfume:
Before each lucid pannel fuming stood
A censer fed with myrrh and spiced wood,
Each by a sacred tripod held aloft,
Whose slender feet wide-swerv'd upon the soft
Wool-woofed carpets: fifty wreaths of smoke
From fifty censers their light voyage took
To the high roof, still mimick'd as they rose
Along the mirror'd walls by twin-clouds odorous.
Twelve sphered tables, by silk seats insphered,
High as the level of a man's breast rear'd
On libbard's paws, upheld the heavy gold
Of cups and goblets, . . .
                (II, 125-31, 138-41, 173-86)

Lamia's architectural preference is for prominently symmetrical vertical lines (tree-stems, tripods, rectangular marble panels) and circles (rising wreaths of smoke, raised circular tables surrounded by silk seats, spherical cups and goblets). The mock-basilica ambience is obvious; indeed, the "aisled place" suggests a bold persepctive with its vanishing point at some unmentionable (sacrificial?) altar. In short, just as the rational philosopher Apollonius seems at the dénouement to practice a kind of "Unlawful magic" (" 'Shut, shut those juggling eyes, thou ruthless man!' " [II, 286, 277]), so the magical Lamia seems here an almost Newtonian designer, as if she were unconsciously providing precisely the ambience for her enforced disappearance.

It is Apollonius' reductive rationalism, of course, that prompts the narrator's scorn in the subsequent "wreath passage":

                . . . and, for the sage,
Let spear-grass and spiteful thistle wage
War on his temples. Do not all charms fly

At the mere touch of cold philosophy?
There was an awful rainbow once in heaven:
We know her woof, her texture; she is given
In the dull catalogue of common things.
Philosophy will clip an Angel's wings,
Conquer all mysteries by rule and line,
Empty the haunted air, and gnomed mine—
Unweave a rainbow, as it erewhile made
The tender-person'd Lamia melt into a shade.
                              (II, 228-38)

But Apollonius is not the only unweaver of nature in the poem; [15] Lamia, we have been told, is "of sciential brain" and can ". . . unperplex bliss from its neighbour pain; / Define their pettish limits, and estrange / Their points of contact, and swift counterchange; / Intrigue with the specious chaos, and dispart / Its most ambiguous atoms with sure art" (I, 191-96).

In short, the poem provides much evidence that each one is both a magician and a rational "designer." This covert correlation of the personalitites of these two ultimate enemies is important because it renders the seemingly absolute derogation of Apollonius in the "wreath passage" highly equivocal. That is, the negative judgment of him is simultaneously true and untrue. Only a part of Keats's mind, the "dull brain," can accept it; only readers who want a strict moral from *Lamia* will seize upon it. Lycius' guardian and teacher defies our attempts at moral evaluation at least as effectively as does his alternately rapacious and victimized deceiver. Throughout *Lamia* the proliferating ambiguities first excite but finally exhaust the reader's imagination, and this is deliberate; Keats artfully portrays an unstable, disintegrating imaginative world. Nothing is single or simple; either appearances are deceiving, or personality is so various that it seems without defining limits or an identifiable base. Hence the characters' peculiar metamorphoses and abrupt shifts in behavior.

Apollonius' magical power to destroy love proves stronger than Lamia's to preserve it, and her withering disappearance under his stern glare reenacts the *reductio ad nihilum* of her sham-metamorphosis. Her eyes lose recognition, she becomes mute, her vibrant beauty fades: "all was blight; / Lamia, no longer fair, there sat a deadly white" (II, 275-76). When Apollonius, who has solved the knotty problem of her former incarnation, actually names it— " 'And shall I see thee made a serpent's prey?' " (II, 298)—she vanishes with a frightful scream.[16] We are not told what new form she will now take, but in any case it is important to realize that she does not die (rather, she "melt[s] into a shade"). As if she were some weird sister of Keats's nightingale, she was "not born for death"; that is the fate reserved for the mortal Lycius who, unlike the speaker of the ode, is incapable of recovering from his extraordinary experience. That is, he is unable to die into a new life of more sober understanding; instead, he simply becomes a sod:

> And Lycius's arms were empty of delight,
> As were his limbs of life, from that same night.
> On the high couch he lay!—his friends came round—
> Supported him—no pulse, or breath they found,
> And, in its marriage robe, the heavy body wound.
>   (II, 307-11)

This is the poem's most cynical dramatic event: Keats's refusal to grant Lycius even a moment's reflection on his disillusionment indicates his anger at the insubstantial nature of visionary experience. Indeed, the pathos of Lamia's evanescence is very nearly swallowed up by its ugliness. Keats's fury also informs Lycius' hysterical denunciation of Apollonius at the close, as well as his portrait of the old sage himself throughout the poem.[17] He is gruff and splenetic because the poet can barely control his frustration at Apollonius' cruel yet morally necessary behavior. The cold philosopher embodies the pain of truth as Keats then felt it, and he lives on, unpleasantly.[18]

The ubiquitous metamorphoses in *Lamia* can be appreciated only when they are compared to their counterparts elsewhere in Keats's poetry. Excluding, as we are explicitly told to do, the experience of the purely immortal Hermes and the nymph (which in any case parodies ideal fulfillment), the transformations in this poem are either unnatural, specious, or fatal. None yields higher moral awareness, in part because the realms in which such awareness might be enacted (Lamia's visionary world of erotic bliss, the life for which Apollonius wishes to save Lycius) are portrayed as unbearable. *Lamia* is a poem without any viable locus of positive value. Hence its metamorphoses are perforce corrupt. Therein lies the poem's ultimate cynicism.

Notes

1. Gittings, *John Keats*, p. 338.
2. Sir Sidney Colvin lamented that "the one fundamental flaw in *Lamia* concerns its moral. The word is crude: what I mean is the bewilderment in which it leaves us as to the effect intended to be made on our imaginative sympathies." Referring to the well-known "wreath passage" in Part II, he says: "These lines to my mind have not only the fault of breaking the story at a critical point and anticipating its issue, but challenge the mind to untimely questionings and reflections. The wreaths of ominous growth distributed to each of the three personages may symbolize the general tragedy: but why are we asked to take sides with the enchantress, ignoring everything about her except her charm, and against the sage? If she were indeed a thing of bale under a mask of beauty, was not the friend and tutor bound to unmask her? and if the pupil could not survive the loss of his illusion,—if he could not confront the facts of life and build up for himself a new happiness on a surer foundation—was it not better that he should be let perish? Is there not in all this a slackening of imaginative and intellectual grasp?" (*John Keats: His Life and Poetry, His Friends, Critics, and After-Fame* [New York: Charles Scribner's Sons, 1917], pp. 408, 409).

   Answering Colvin, John Middleton Murry declares: "The reason why we are asked to take sides with the enchantress in *Lamia* is that Keats was in love with her. The truth about the Lamia is that Keats himself did not know whether she was a thing of beauty or a thing of bale." Murry has no doubt that the poem "is imaginative autobiography, and of the most exact and faithful kind. Keats is Lycius, Fanny Brawne is the Lamia, and Apollonius is Charles Brown the realist, trying to break Fanny's spell over Keats by insisting upon her as the female animal. The identification seems transparent" (*Keats and Shakespeare*, pp. 159, 157). Echoing Murry's contention that Keats could not make up his mind, Douglas Bush writes that *Lamia* "takes its place among the many poems which embody the inward struggle between the claims of self and the senses and the claims of the world and 'philosophy.' But here Keats does not seem to know which side he is on, and a plausible case can be, and has been, made out for *Lamia* as a condemnation of philosophy, as a condemnation of the senses, and as a condemnation of a divorce between the two. Each of these interpretations can be supported by chapter and verse from Keats's other poems and from his letters, yet each leaves difficulties in *Lamia* itself" *(Mythology and the Romantic Tradition in English Poetry,* p. 110). For Bush, the source of the difficulty is ultimately biographical: ". . . the fire that Keats was aware of in *Lamia* was not merely born of opposed literary desires, however intense, it came from the divided soul of a lover. The struggle between passion and the craving to escape from passion is felt too keenly and rendered too literally . . . to result in a unified, integrated poem" (p. 112).

Though basing his estimate not on biography but on Keats's choice and handling of symbols, James Boulger has more recently spoken of the poem's confusion: "the emotional commitment is not entirely at one with the intellectual" ("Keats' Symbolism," 252). E. C. Pettet and David Perkins follow Bush, though they do not claim that the poem's ambiguity constitutes an aesthetic failure. Pettet notes that Keats "cannot achieve a mood of calm acceptance. He, the poet, is himself a young man of passionate feelings desperately entangled in love, and he cannot but feel bitterly regretful, even resentful, that the charm must indeed fly" *(On the Poetry of Keats* [Cambridge, Eng.: Cambridge Univ. Press, 1957], pp. 239-40); Perkins senses "an irresolution in Keats himself," adding that though the poem reveals "a more settled state of mind" than do the odes, there is doubt on Keats's part over "what attitude to take in exposing the visionary imagination" symbolized by Lamia *(The Quest for Permanence,* p. 264). But Pettet and Perkins, while fully cognizant of the poem's ambiguities, still see it as dramatizing a definite theme: "Keats is posing an unhappy dilemma [between dreams and undeluded truth], but it is not the core of the poem. Instead the poem is largely about the consequences of being a dreamer" (Perkins, *The Quest for Permanence,* p. 273); ". . . in *Lamia,* above everything else, he is expressing the idea that love is an ultimately destructive force because its world is one of illusion and unreality" (Pettet, *On the Poetry of Keats,* p. 237; see also Walter Evert, *Aesthetic and Myth in the Poetry of Keats* [Princeton, N.J.: Princeton Univ. Press, 1965], pp. 275-76).

Finally, there is a large group of critics who view the poem's unresolved ambiguities as purposeful, according to the criterion of verisimilitude. For example, Earl Wasserman writes that "most examinations of the poem have centered on the relation of Lamia and Apollonius, and therefore have searched for the relation of values they appear to represent, as though Keats were defending sensuous beauty against philosophy, or philosophy against sensuous beauty. The repeated failure to find any solution to this problem results, I believe, from the fact that there is no problem. Rather, the legend of Lycius and Lamia is an account of what needs must happen to mortal man's aspirations, not an evaluation of what inspires and destroys them . . ." *(The Finer Tone,* p. 163). Similarly, Bernard Blackstone comments that "Critics have questioned Keats's art in the conclusion of the poem. They want a clear-cut moral. Keats doesn't give them one, because he is not describing what ought to be, but what is. The situation, like the situations of life itself, is too involved for a neat solution" (*The Consecrated Urn*, pp. 305-6; see also Bernice Slote, *Keats and the Dramatic Principle* [Lincoln, Neb.: Univ. of Nebraska Press, 1958], p. 140; Miriam Allott, " 'Isabella,' 'The Eve of St. Agnes,' and 'Lamia,' " in *John Keats: A Reassessment*, ed. Kenneth Muir, pp. 59, 63; Gittings, *John Keats*, pp. 337-38; and Sperry, *Keats the Poet*, p. 309). It should also be noted that, in addition to several critics cited above, two of Keats's recent biographers see the poet's involvement with Fanny Brawne as in some sense bearing upon the poem, as Murry had insisted, though their handling of the biographical context is far more judicious than his. See Bate, *John Keats*, p. 544, and Ward, *John Keats: The Making of a Poet*, p. 308.

3. Sperry, in his stimulating discussion of the poem, notes "a bitterness verging at times on sarcasm, a disconcerting quality of self-mockery" (*Keats the Poet*, p. 292).

4. Boulger calls the Hermes episode "sportive": "It is not ideal love. [Hermes] has a reputation among the gods as a successful rake. Also, noted for his ability to drive a hard bargain, he usually gets the better of his female friends in love contests. This explains to a certain extent his dealings with the Lamia, for he clearly prospered by their arrangement, while she suffered. The nymph is a much weaker figure than the god, a pawn in his game with Lamia, and of no significance for a scheme of ideal love" ("Keats' Symbolism," 250). Similarly, Richard Benvenuto comments that "Hermes is not an ideal by which the rest of the poem judges Lycius. . . . He does not bring a new morality to bear upon life in an amoral universe. His adventures are themselves a slice of that universe . . ." (" 'The Ballance of Good and Evil' in Keats's Letters and in 'Lamia'," *Journal of English and Germanic Philology*, 71 [1972]: 9).

5. M. Allott, in *Keats: The Complete Poems*, notes that "Hermes was renowned for his specious eloquence" and quotes Lemprière: " 'He . . . not only presided over orators, merchants, and declaimers, but was also the god of thieves, pick-pockets, and all dishonest persons . . .' " (p. 620fn).

6. Bate, *John Keats*, p. 554.

7. "The description resembles nothing so much as the effects of a violent chemical reaction. Both in what it depicts and what it implies, the passage is marked by a brilliant, mocking irony" (Sperry, *Keats the Poet*, p. 301).

8. "To compare the fiery pangs of Lamia's etherealization to the 'fierce convulse' and 'wild commotions' of Apollo's dying into life at the end of *Hyperion* is to understand how a serious conception had become a subject for deliberate travesty" (Sperry, *Keats the Poet*, p. 302).

9. See *Keats: The Complete Poems*, ed. M. Allott, p. 626fn.

10. Boulger notes that "When Lycius met Lamia he was prepared for a symbolic flight of some kind; . . . he had allowed his reason to fade into the twilight of the dream world. In other words he bore some secret, perhaps unrecognized, grudge against his educational training with Apollonius. Lamia offered a way out of the dreary sensible world and he took it" ("Keats' Symbolism," p. 253).

11. "The reader sees that the relationship between Lycius and Lamia is created by magic, by deception, in short, by a witch. The relationship emphasizes physical, sexual, yet not entirely sensual, love. It avoids love melancholy and pain . . . ," yet it "contains no element of the divine. It is human love supported by magic, for only by illusion can it avoid the difficulties of mortal passion" (Boulger, "Keats' Symbolism," p. 251).

12. Blackstone's discussion (*The Consecrated Urn*, pp. 299-305), is particularly helpful here.

13. There are many other significant contrasts between the two poems. Porphyro's stratagem is ultimately beneficial; Lycius' proposal is disastrous. Angela, the guardian angel, is comically ineffectual; Apollonius, the paternalistic sage, is all too effective. Porphyro and Madeline are safely sheltered from the raucous crowd; Lycius and Lamia come to grief in the herd's presence. The seemingly magical sliding of bolts and so forth at the close of *The Eve of St. Agnes* works for the protagonists; magic at the end of *Lamia* destroys the lovers.

14. Indeed, nothing could be more incongruous with the poem's shadowy texture than these boldly colored valuations. Sperry notes that "The poet's invitation to the reader to join him in choosing and awarding wreaths to the three principals is partly tongue-in-cheek and partly a deliberate trap. For any reasoned balance of sympathies, not to mention taking sides, is out of the question. The characters and the attitudes they represent are all hopelessly inadequate" (*Keats the Poet*, p. 309).

15. Bate points out the constricted meaning of "Philosophy" that Apollonius represents: it is "limited to the reductive uses of analytic philosophy, the essence of which is to reduce a thing to certain elements and then to substitute the simple interpretation for the original complex reality. What is not susceptible of such reduction is merely denied" (*John Keats*, p. 559).

16. The point about naming is made by Boulger ("Keats' Symbolism," p. 253).

17. Benvenuto points out the irony inherent in Lycius' denunciation of his master: "In his opposition . . . Lycius uses the same reductionistic rhetoric against Apollonius that Apollonius uses against Lamia. He accuses the old man of 'impious proud-heart sophistries, / Unlawful magic, and enticing lies.' He tries to make Apollonius the devil, speaks of his 'demon eyes,' and calls down the vengeance of the gods. If Lycius is the victim of anyone's magic, it is Lamia's; and if he is, it is largely a willful self-delusion" (" 'The Ballance of Good and Evil' . . . ," p. 7).

18. Bate notes that Apollonius alone survives, and adds that "he is given throughout an impressive dignity lacking in the others" (*John Keats*, p. 560).

7.

The Fall of Hyperion: Immortal Steps

This morning Poetry has conquered—I have relapsed into those abstractions which are my only life—I feel escaped from a new strange and threatening sorrow.—And I am thankful for it—There is an awful warmth about my heart like a load of immortality.

        —Letter to J. H. Reynolds, 22 (?) September 1818

This living hand, now warm and capable
Of earnest grasping, would, if it were cold
And in the icy silence of the tomb,
So haunt thy days and chill thy dreaming nights
That thou would wish thine own heart dry of blood,
So in my veins red life might stream again,
And thou be conscience-calm'd. See, here it is—
I hold it towards you.

From one point of view, *The Fall of Hyperion* is a deep meditation on all the metamorphoses (save those in *Lamia)* to be found in

Keats's previous poetry. In particular, it attempts to probe and thereby widen the context of Apollo's dying into life in the first *Hyperion;* under the influence of Dante's *Purgatorio,* epic is transformed into vision in order to reflect, in an austerely pure poetic manner, Keats's most insightful view of the individual human life and of collective human experience.[1] Of course, *The Fall* is a fragment and in strictly formal terms must be judged, like the first *Hyperion,* a brilliant failure; as in the first version, the ambitious breadth of Keats's ideas contends with a more limited architectural skill. The poem's difficulties have been well stated elsewhere and will not be discussed here.[2] Rather, without at all claiming a submerged formal unity in the fragment, I want to focus on the metamorphic episodes in the narrative, which constitute a kind of continuity and which I believe express the essence of the poem's meaning.

The thought contained in the poem's short Induction is compressed, and its full range of implication can be grasped only in the light of the dialogue between the dreamer (obviously Keats's persona) and Moneta later on. The Induction's seminal idea is that "every man whose soul is not a clod / Hath visions, and would speak, if he had lov'd / And been well nurtured in his mother tongue" (I, 13-15). Unfortunately, the dreams of fanatic and savage do not last, because they are not "Trac'd upon vellum or wild Indian leaf"; "For Poesy alone can tell her dreams, / With the fine spell of words alone can save / Imagination from the sable charm / And dumb enchantment" (I, 5, 8-11).[3] The real issue, then, is the endurance of the poetic dream, its eternal presence. But when, in the Induction's last three lines, the dreamer speaks personally, the terms of the argument are subtly altered:

> Whether the dream now purposed to rehearse
> Be poet's or fanatic's will be known
> When this warm scribe my hand is in the grave.
> > (I, 16-18)

Here the distinction between poet and fanatic cannot possibly be a matter of putting the dream into words, for the warm scribe his hand is doing just that; rather, it implicitly raises the issue of value. This dream will endure if future generations (not just the fanatic's "sect") judge it worthy. Only then can it lay claim to being a genuine poet's dream; if it is deficient, it will go the evanescent way of the fanatic's and the savage's, despite its having been written down. The Induction is consistent with the later dialogue insofar as Keats doubts in both his status as true poet; only in the dialogue does he consider what constitutes worthy—and hence lasting—verse. But, again, the real issue of the Induction, emphasized in its concluding three lines, is the endurance of the poetic dream.

During the first stage of his reverie, the dreamer finds himself in a luxurious garden, whose "trees of every clime" and "arbour with a drooping roof / Of trellis vines, and bells, and larger blooms, / Like floral-censers swinging light in air" (I, 19, 25-27) recall all such bowers in his verse, from the 1817 *Poems* through the "Psyche" and "Nightingale" odes. It is the realm of Flora and old Pan that Keats predicted, in "Sleep and Poetry," he would have to "pass . . . for a nobler life, / Where I may find the agonies, the strife / Of human hearts"; it is the Chamber of Maiden-Thought, where "we become intoxicated with the light and the atmosphere, we see nothing but pleasant wonders . . ." (I, 281). "A feast of summer fruits" is spread before him, more plentiful than Ceres' "fabled horn" could pour forth for Proserpine's annual return; but this abundance is curiously qualified: the feast, when "nearer seen, seem'd refuse of a meal / By angel tasted, or our mother Eve; / For empty shells were scattered on the grass, / And grape stalks but half bare, and remnants more, / Sweet smelling, whose pure kinds I could not know" (I, 29, 35, 30-34). The dreamer is literally taking a closer look at the bower world, and he finds that it is a place that creatures vanish from, not, apparently, where they can endure. Indeed, his sojourn there is brief, for having satiated the hunger and thirst that the bower stimulated in him, he is transported to an altogether different world, the austere and somber realm of Saturn's temple, whose "black gates / Were shut against the sunrise evermore" (I, 85-86).[4] Keats's symbolic judgment of a poetry that merely images the world's sensory delights is clear and absolute: though attractive, it must be abandoned when one has had one's fill. Correlatively, poetry that celebrates exclusively such a world is a "refuse" of human experience and deserves to endure only as a remnant, a pleasing memory.

The dreamer's flight from garden to temple, which of course signals a transformation of subjective awareness, seems to be Keats's self-conscious evocation of Endymion's travels. Here, however, the initiating discontent is not sexual longing but a literal hunger and thirst: ". . . appetite / More yearning than on earth I ever felt . . ." (I, 38-39). The "full draught" he imbibes "is parent of my theme" (I, 46), and its immediate effect is to engender a deathlike "cloudy swoon":

> No Asian poppy, nor elixir fine
> Of the soon fading jealous caliphat;
> No poison gender'd in close monkish cell,
> To thin the scarlet conclave of old men,
> Could so have rapt unwilling life away.
> Among the fragrant husks and berries crush'd,
> Upon the grass I struggled hard against
> The domineering potion; but in vain:
> The cloudy swoon came on, and down I sunk
> Like a Silenus on an antique vase.
>
> (I, 47-56)

And the cloudy swoon gives way to a new, more elevated consciousness, imaged in part by a simile of upward flight:

> How long I slumber'd 'tis a chance to guess.
> When sense of life return'd, I started up
> As if with wings; but the fair trees were gone,
> The mossy mound and arbour were no more.
>
> (I, 57-60)

Significantly, the dreamer resists his transformative experience, fearing that its outcome will be death. This resistance suggests the travail of exploring life's dark chambers; it also prefigures the poem's most compelling event. For during his subsequent dying into life on the altar stairs, the dreamer's struggle against the domi-

neering Moneta's fatal threat will be even more intense, because
the final achievement of visionary awareness—taking on Wordsworth's "burden of the Mystery"—is far more strenuous than his
mere journeying from garden to temple.

The enormous "old sanctuary with roof august" (I, 62) in which
the dreamer now finds himself is, in Murry's memorable phrase,
"the temple of life become conscious of itself in man." [5] Just as the
garden was planted with "trees of every clime," so are this "eternal
domed monument" (I, 71) and its accoutrements, as Bloom notes,
a blending of "five religious traditions—Christian, Jewish, Egyp-
tian, Olympian, Druidic—because [Keats] wants the abandoned
temple of Saturn to represent the shrine of religious consciousness
itself," which outlasts the sovereignty of its particular forms: "All
in a mingled heap confus'd there lay / Robes, golden tongs, censer,
and chafing-dish, / Girdles, and chains, and holy jewelries" (I, 78-
80).[6] The vast expanse in which the temple is centered suggests
Keats's own vale of soulmaking, where the intelligence is schooled
through awareness of the world's misery, soon to be proved by the
dreamer quite literally on his pulses. Schooling begins with visual
assimilation:

> . . . once more I rais'd
> My eyes to fathom the space every way;
> The embossed roof, the silent massy range
> Of columns north and south, ending in mist
> Of nothing, then to eastward, where black gates
> Were shut against the sunrise evermore.
> Then to the west I look'd, and saw far off
> An image. . . .
>
> (I, 81-88)

The dreamer's progress is, as Ward notes, "from east to west, in the
direction of earthly time itself," suggesting that subsequent events
will deal with matters of mortality, though under the aspect of
eternity.[7] Such had been the theme of the final lines of the poem's
Induction.

As the dreamer stands at the foot of the shrine, his transition
from garden to temple is symbolically reiterated in a way that

underscores the impermanence of the purely sensuous world he has left behind. The shrine's sacrificial fire sends forth "Maian incense," which "spread around / Forgetfulness of everything but bliss"; the smoke is compared to the odor of spring flowers that "fills the air with so much pleasant health / That even the dying man forgets his shroud" (I, 100-104). But the incense's healthful, narcotic effect is only momentary, for from out of the cloud comes Moneta's severe challenge. The dying man cannot, after all, forget his shroud.

> "If thou canst not ascend
> These steps, die on that marble where thou art.
> Thy flesh, near cousin to the common dust,
> Will parch for lack of nutriment—thy bones
> Will wither in few years, and vanish so
> That not the quickest eye could find a grain
> Of what thou now art on that pavement cold.
> The sands of thy short life are spent this hour,
> And no hand in the universe can turn
> Thy hour glass, if these gummed leaves be burnt
> Ere thou canst mount up these immortal steps."
>   (I, 107-17)

Stunned by "that fierce threat, and the hard task proposed" (I, 120), the dreamer hesitates:

> . . . suddenly a palsied chill
> Struck from the paved level up my limbs,
> And was ascending quick to put cold grasp
> Upon those streams that pulse beside the throat:
> I shriek'd; and the sharp anguish of my shriek
> Stung my own ears—I strove hard to escape
> The numbness; strove to gain the lowest step.
> Slow, heavy, deadly was my pace: the cold
> Grew stifling, suffocating, at the heart;
> And when I clasp'd my hands I felt them not.
> One minute before death, my iced foot touch'd
> The lowest stair; and as it touch'd, life seem'd

To pour in at the toes: I mounted up,
As once fair Angels on a ladder flew
From the green turf to heaven.

(I, 122-36)

The dreamer's palsied chill, his hard striving to escape the numbness, and his angelic ascent are all intensifications of his previous
cloudy swoon, his struggle against the domineering potion, his
starting up as if with wings; literally and figuratively, he has only
now achieved the vantage point of vision. The episode is also a
more insightful revision of Apollo's dying into life. For the god's
"wild commotions . . . made flush / All the immortal fairness of his
limbs"; that is, his hot pangs seemed to enhance his beauty: "His
very hair, his golden tresses famed, / Kept undulation round
his eager neck." By contrast, there is nothing attractive in the
dreamer's numbness, suffocation, and near paralysis; indeed, the
exaggerated reference to physiological detail—"limbs," "throat,"
"ears," "heart," "hands," "foot," "toes"—makes his experience appear ugly and repulsive.[8] Devoid of any ideal beauty, his suffering
is thoroughly mortal. Finally, whereas Apollo's deification oc-
curred almost spontaneously, the dreamer is compelled to *act* by
Moneta's tyrannous threat of extinction. Of the two, he is the more
resolute and persevering: "I strove hard to escape / The numbness;
strove to gain the lowest step." Though diseased, he heals himself
through his own strenuous effort. He earns his new life.

In other words, the dreamer wins the race against time—*his* hand
turns the hourglass, or, as Moneta puts it, " 'Thou hast felt / What
'tis to die and live again before / Thy fated hour. That thou hadst
power to do so / Is thy own safety; thou hast dated on / Thy
doom' " (I, 141-45). When coupled with the reward of visionary
insight that follows, the dreamer's victory over time implicitly declares the value of his dreaming, its worthiness to endure. The
declaration is implicit because, as his dialogue with Moneta shows,
the dreamer is beset with self-doubt over the nature of his role and
the value of imaginative creation generally.

But the symbolic drama of climbing the stairs is apparently only
another stage in the dreamer's quest toward vision. Having endured Moneta's challenge to his physical being, he must now

contend with her intellectually before the Titans' story will be
revealed to him. It is as if the dreamer's ascent of the altar stairs
proves him to be imaginative only in the lowest degree. There is no
real point of repose in *The Fall of Hyperion;* that is, the events of the
poem never resolve the dreamer's yearning but, rather, propel him
relentlessly to new heights or depths of understanding. Thus, in the
much debated passage of Canto I (187-210), which the scrupulous
Woodhouse says Keats "seems to have intended to erase" but
which is vital to the poem's development,[9] the dreamer rather
compulsively urges Moneta to expatiate upon her accusation that
he is merely " 'a dreaming thing; / A fever of thyself' " (I, 168-69):

> "If it please,
> Majestic shadow, tell me: sure not all
> Those melodies sung into the world's ear
> Are useless: sure a poet is a sage;
> A humanist, physician to all men.
> That I am none I feel, as vultures feel
> They are no birds when eagles are abroad.
> What am I then? Thou spakest of my tribe:
> What tribe?" . . .
>   "Art thou not of the dreamer tribe?
> The poet and the dreamer are distinct,
> Diverse, sheer opposite, antipodes.
> The one pours out a balm upon the world,
> The other vexes it."
>   (I, 186-94; 198-202)

The medical diction is crucial. It carries us all the way back to "I
stood tip-toe," where the sick who are magically cured celebrate
their new and healthy lives by loosening their tongues in poesy:
"Therefore no lover did of anguish die: / But the soft numbers, in
that moment spoken, / Made silken ties, that never may be broken." In the dialogue between the dreamer and Moneta, one must
admire Keats's courageous probing of imaginative self-absorption
and distraction, but my feeling is that the process of self-curing
that occurs on the altar steps makes clear that Keats *did* consider
himself a physician to all men, capable of pouring out a balm upon

the world.[10] In other words, all the dreamer's self-accusations in the dialogue are valuable insofar as they record an important aspect of Keats's honesty and constitute a further stage in the dreamer's quest for the privilege of vision. However, I would argue that the dialogue, with its rather uncharacteristic consecutive reasoning, seems much less imaginatively compelling than either the dreamer's successful ascent of the altar stairs or his subsequent vision of Moneta's face, both of which are derived from the idea of metamorphosis.[11]

After the dialogue, Moneta ceases to function as the poet's conscience and takes on an independent emblematic role. It is of some importance to note that the priestess is most communicative *after* she offers to reveal the wondrous " 'scenes / Still swooning vivid through my globed brain' " (I, 244-45)—that is, when she ceases to interrogate and falls silent:

> Then saw I a wan face,
> Not pin'd by human sorrows, but bright blanch'd
> By an immortal sickness which kills not;
> It works a constant change, which happy death
> Can put no end to; deathwards progressing
> To no death was that visage; it had pass'd
> The lily and the snow; and beyond these
> I must not think now, though I saw that face—
> But for her eyes I should have fled away.
> They held me back, with a benignant light,
> Soft mitigated by divinest lids
> Half closed, and visionless entire they seem'd
> Of all external things—they saw me not,
> But in blank splendor beam'd like the mild moon,
> Who comforts those she sees not, who knows not
> What eyes are upward cast.
>
> (I, 256-71)

Beautifully austere, Moneta's face discloses "constant change"— perpetual metamorphosis—under the aspect of eternity; process and permanence cease to contend, having been united in a mysterious integrity. Its sickness is immortal, unable to end in "happy death" but, rather, progressing to a state beyond it ("Past / The lily and the snow"). It is a sorrowfully wan face in its eternal suffering, but ultimately one that comforts "with a benignant light" because it proclaims suffering to be universal, the very condition of humanity. Within the poem, this image is both prefigurative and retrospective; that is, Moneta faces in all directions, as befits her immortal rank. Her agony both epitomizes the Titans' forthcoming history and sums up preceding events centered on the dreamer. For there exists a symbolic intimacy between Moneta's expression and his dying into life, hinted at when he says of the priestess's voice: "As near as an immortal's sphered words / Could to a mother's soften, were these last" (I, 249-50). That is, this eternalized tableau and the preceding symbolic drama are in reality two versions of the same imaginative impulse, and they serve to illuminate one another. Thus, just as Moneta embodies the continual suffering of all ages, which makes her sickness immortal, so had the dreamer's discrete agony given him a kind of immortality; it had "dated on" his doom. Similarly, just as Moneta's visage progresses "deathwards . . . / To no death" but ultimately beams forth a "benignant light," so had the dreamer moved toward death, only to live again and tell the Titans' story—that is, to become a true poet and pour out "a balm upon the world" by himself revealing the universality of sorrow. Thus Moneta's face is an abstraction of human fate subsuming cycles of individual existence, which do indeed end, but which together constitute the destiny of the race. Full of beauty, dignity, and pain, it is also Keats's supreme symbol of poetry itself, a poetry that would brave the misery of human life and "which happy death / Can put no end to," a poetry that comforts those it sees not, nor knows what eyes are cast upon it.[12]

But however enlightening, this gazing brings little comfort to the dreamer himself. Rather, it makes him greedy for the knowledge that molds Moneta's vision:

> As I had found
> A grain of gold upon a mountain's side,
> And ting'd with avarice strain'd out my eyes
> To search its sullen entrails rich with ore,

So at the view of sad Moneta's brow,
I ached to see what things the hollow brain
Behind enwombed: what high tragedy
In the dark secret chambers of her skull
Was acting, that could give so dread a stress
To her cold lips, and fill with such a light
Her planetary eyes; and touch her voice
With such a sorrow.

                        (I, 271-82)

He is rewarded with "A Power . . . of enormous ken, / To see as a God sees, and take the depth / Of things as nimbly as the outward eye / Can size and shape pervade" (I, 303-6); but the knowledge is once again torturous, nearly annihilating. The new life of vision, like Moneta's visage, is itself deathward progressing to no death.

                    Without stay or prop
But my own weak mortality, I bore
The load of this eternal quietude,
The unchanging gloom, and the three fixed shapes
Ponderous upon my senses a whole moon.
For by my burning brain I measured sure
Her silver seasons shedded on the night,
And every day by day methought I grew
More gaunt and ghostly. Oftentimes I pray'd
Intense, that death would take me from the vale
And all its burthens. Gasping with despair
Of change, hour after hour I curs'd myself.

                        (I, 388-99)

For all his pain, the poet perseveres and begins to tell his tale. But not for long. The fragment would become the fit emblem for a fragmented life, and Keats, the enduring poet of spiritual change, would become one with Moneta herself.

Notes

1. For the Dantean influence on the poem, see J. L. Lowes, *"Hyperion* and the *Purgatorio," Times Literary Supplement,* January 11, 1936, p. 35. Gittings comments on the retrospective quality of the lines preceding the Titans' story: "In the opening to the new poem, Keats ranged through the best of all his hard-won poetic experiences, from youthful Spenserian freshness to the tempered finality of his latest work, bringing all to an essential harmony. There are clear traces from all of the four great odes he had just decided to keep for his book; the imagery of a feast enjoyed before some decisive experience was repeated, as it had been in every narrative poem since *The Eve of St. Agnes"* (*John Keats,* pp. 341-42).

2. For various interpretations of the ambiguous dialogue between the dreamer and Moneta, see Murry, *Keats and Shakespeare,* pp. 176ff.; Brian Wicker, "The Disputed Lines in *The Fall of Hyperion," Essays in Criticism,* 7 (1957): 28-41; and James Land Jones, *Adam's Dream: Mythic Consciousness in Keats and Yeats* (Athens, Ga.: Univ. of Georgia Press, 1975), pp. 189-93, a most cogent sorting-out of the difficulties. Harold Bloom has given a succinct explanation of why the poem remains a fragment: "Keats's problem . . . is precisely the reverse of the problem that caused him to abandon *Hyperion,* and one may wonder whether a solution was possible in either poem. In *Hyperion,* Keats began with the myth of the fall of Saturn, and had to manage a transition to his personal myth of poetic incarnation. In the *Fall,* he began with his own dying into the life of tragic poetry, and next had to externalize this theme into its affinities with the story of the Titans. But the affinities are strained, and the Titanic myth is irrelevant to Keats's more intense concerns. Apollo is really all Keats needs for his own myth, and so *The Fall of Hyperion* tends to break into two poems . . ." (*The Visionary Company,* p. 451).

   David Perkins has provided the best summary of the issues Keats raises in *The Fall* and suggests credibly why they are not resolved: "There is the suspicion that he has been a dreamer, the assertion that he ought not to be, and the fear that poetry may inevitably involve illusion and make-believe. There is the notion that the poet has special powers of vision beyond those of other men, and the contrary premise that all men have visions like the poet. There is the assumption that the poet stands apart from the typical life of man, and the wish to see him as a humanitarian actively engaged in promoting human welfare. Finally, there is the desire to find some 'haven,' and the conviction that it cannot be found, especially by the poet. Of course, *The Fall of Hyperion* does not simply pose these questions; it attempts to resolve them, but in doing so it partially abandons an indirect, symbolic approach and proceeds more by statement and didactic assertion. The result is unfortunate. One can scarcely hope to lead a forward march of argument until a mass of contrary sympathies has been ordered, disciplined, and purged. In *The Fall of Hyperion,* the ferment in Keats's mind produced as much confusion as complexity" *(The Quest for Permanence,* p. 277).

3. As Murry notes, the thought here is compressed because Keats defines poetry in two ways, "as utterance making dreams immortal, and as a condition of soul" *(Keats and Shakespeare,* p. 171).

4. Cf. Keats's comments on our eventual departure from the Chamber of Maiden-Thought, where "we become intoxicated with the light and the atmosphere, we see nothing but pleasant wonders, and think of delaying there for ever in delight: However among the effects this breathing is father of is that tremendous one of sharpening one's vision into the heart and nature of Man—of convincing ones nerves that the World is full of Misery and Heartbreak, Pain, Sickness and oppression—whereby This Chamber of Maiden Thought becomes gradually darken'd and at the same time on all sides of it many doors are set open—but all dark—all leading to dark passages . . ." *(Letters,* I, 281).

5. John Middleton Murry, *Keats and Shakespeare,* p. 174.

6. Bloom, *The Visionary Company,* p. 444.

7. Ward, *John Keats: The Making of a Poet,* p. 326.

8. Bate points out that "in combination with the use of the remote and abstract as background is a new, sharply analytic consciousness of the body as an anatomical event both brief and complex. Thus, at the start, we find the narrator aware of his own hand as he writes, and thinking ahead to the cold that is to come. . . . Empathy is focused on the physical functions of the body; the tongue seeking to find syllables 'about its roofed home'; terror that makes the 'heart too small to hold its blood'; the massive chill that rises from the pavement through the limbs 'to put cold grasp / Upon those streams that pulse beside the throat'; the strained effort to penetrate the dark 'chambers' of Moneta's brain . . ." *(John Keats,* p. 592).

9. See the textual note in Stillinger, *The Poems of John Keats,* p. 672.

10. Ward writes that "The self-cured physician here becomes Keats's image of redemption through poetry. By confronting his own sickness, Keats implies, the dreamer may at last surmount it, become a true poet who does not 'vex' mankind with dreams of unreal happiness but heals it through his own understanding of 'the giant agony of the world' " *(John Keats: The Making of a Poet,* p. 328).

11. Perhaps the dreamer's most perplexing self-accusation is contained in Moneta's eulogy to the simple life of labor, with the neat division of affects it supposedly inspires: " 'Every sole man hath days of joy and pain, / Whether his labours be sublime or low— / The pain alone; the joy alone; distinct' " (I, 172-74). But such a condition abrogates what is perhaps the central psychological insight of all Keats's poetry. Bate notes that "one of Keats's basic premises, deepening with every half year of his development, is the inseparability of joy and pain to the awake and honest consciousness (the Shakespearean 'bittersweet,' mentioned in the sonnet on Lear). The song of Apollo,

representing the new poetry, the more discerning world to come, had made Clymene, in the first *Hyperion,* '*sick / Of joy and grief at once*'; in the yet undiscovered regions mentioned in the 'Ode to Psyche,' the branching thoughts will bring new pleasure and pain simultaneously; the interplay of joy and pain is used dramatically in the 'Nightingale' and as a central theme in 'Melancholy.' Finally, Lamia's magic ability to 'unperplex bliss from its neighbour pain' underlies much of the illusory happiness she inspires: it is exactly this divorce between joy and pain that the outright 'dreamer,' Lycius, craves most and believes he is finding" *(John Keats,* pp. 598-99).

12. No critic has written better on Moneta's face than Murry: "There is unity, there is calm, there is beauty; it is a vision of a single thing. Yet in that single thing what strange elements are combined? Pain, an eternity of pain; change, an eternity of change; death, an eternity of death; terror, yet no terror; instead, measureless benignity; yet this infinite love touches no person; it is eternal and impersonal, 'conforting those it sees not.' That, if the word be accepted, is a great poet's vision of God—but of a godhead immanent in the changing and enduring reality of the world. The mortal poet has gained a more perfect vision of that which was revealed to Apollo. Then he had seen through a glass darkly, but now face to face" *(Keats and Shakespeare,* p. 182).

Epilogue: Metamorphosis in Keats

As we have seen him do elsewhere, Keats uses metamorphosis in *The Fall of Hyperion* to signify his moral and aesthetic progress; at the same time *The Fall* makes very clear why the structural pattern of dying into life was so crucial a part of the poet's imaginative expression. For Keats, to change, to metamorphose, was not-to-die. This is the essential point. To transform one's vision of reality, which for Keats always involved a deeper apprehension of it, was to avoid a kind of spiritual suffocation and paralysis, which he rightly associated with death. This is the key to the poet's astounding technical development over such a brief span of years. Each new poem of any significance required some sort of stylistic change from what he had previously written. Even within so thematically interdependent a group as the spring odes, one finds subtle alterations in stanzaic form and rhyme scheme from poem to poem; it is as if Keats considered exact technical replication a surrender, an aesthetic dying on the stairs of composition.

Metamorphosis, then, both expresses the need for and is the structural paradigm of Keats's continuous process of moral and aesthetic growth. Like all the Romantics, Keats is responding to a politically and philosophically unsettled world, in which revolution—be it social or personal—might lead to new states of understanding and feeling that would transcend the discontents of former times. What sets Keats apart from the other writers of his age is the way in which morbidity figures in his dealing with such issues. The cause of this difference is psychological; that is, the various metamorphoses in Keats's poetry indicate how he was defending one aspect of his being, namely, his creative imagination, from an almost equally potent aspect of mind, namely, his fear of death. Keats's major poems constitute stubborn and heroic imaginative victories over that fear. For all their luxurious sensuousness, the poems pulse with the aggressive energy of a mind confronting and imaginatively working through pain, sickness, oppression, ultimately death itself. This is the real source of the density of affect in Keats's work, of our sense of its rich texture and earnest conviction, even when his stylistic and architectural resources are imperfectly realized. As I maintained at the outset of this study, Keats is by far the most morbid of the six great English Romantics, far more than Byron, whose air of fatality is more often than not mere self-dramatization, though nonetheless resonant for his vast audience. Keats's morbidity, by contrast, is never a pretense; rather, it is the warp of his poetic tapestry, fully inherent.

In addition, there is an erotic component to the Keatsian metamorphosis pattern, which not only complements the poet's unusually sensuous language and his narratives of explicit amorous adventure, but also, through its overt sexual rhythm, partly animates poems that are not primarily about sexual love. We do not distort the "Ode to a Nightingale" by seeing it as a lyric of sublimated eroticism, indicated by its pattern of intense yearning, brief union, followed by fatigue and a return to the ordinary. Similarly, the *Hyperion* poems suggest a process of sexual initiation. Apollo is more evidently the virile youth than is the dreamer of *The Fall*, but both acquire a new sense of reality through the ministrations of knowledgeable female figures. Indeed, the curious vagueness of both Mnemosyne (whom Keats barely describes) and Moneta (who for most of their dialogue is veiled) suggests an emptying and displacement of their inherent eroticism. The initiate's mature awareness is not specifically carnal but is, rather, that of the tragedy inherent in all human process—a suggestive substitution. Thus while the threefold metamorphosis pattern can, in a general way, tell us something of Keats's sexual attitudes in actual love poems like *Endymion, The Eve of St. Agnes,* and *Lamia,* elsewhere it provides an erotic undercurrent, which enhances the urgency of the poet's other moral and aesthetic concerns.

Finally, metamorphosis becomes the means whereby Keats asserts the immortality of poetry. Imaged in Moneta's tragic countenance, "It works a constant change, which happy death / Can put no end to; deathwards progressing / To no death was that visage." This is the poetry Keats has written, with its successive dyings into life—in its mature stages, into a life of tragic apprehension. Process is all for Keats, involving the loss of primitive, often idealistic, states of awareness, which are easily disturbed, and hence felt to be discomforting, by the pressure of circumstance or by an intuitive awareness of some higher knowledge beyond the horizon of consciousness. From his earliest days when he stood tiptoe upon a little hill and saw that "There was a wide wand'ring for the greediest eye, / To peer about upon variety," Keats knew that the voyage was always worth taking, even if the destination were a *terra incognita* or a difficult terrain. We know that his last voyages, to Rome and to death, were difficult indeed.

He rests well in the Eternal City, still comforting those he sees not. The Protestant Cemetery, like all cemeteries, is autumnal even in spring and partakes of the same quiet assurance that Keats poured into his last great poem. "To Autumn" seems in part a reflection off Moneta's face, the metamorphosis of the natural world momentarily glimpsed in its dying time by an eye at once disinterested and alert, melancholy and joyful. As we move through the stages of autumn and from the maturing sun to the soft-dying day, we hear the voice of a man who has made peace with the world. Unlike *The Fall,* the ode is all mental repose. In the final stanza, spring is evoked equivocally—not because it will not return, for life must return—but because it will also pass:

Where are the songs of spring? Ay, where are they?
    Think not of them, thou hast thy music too,—

While barred clouds bloom the soft-dying day,
  And touch the stubble-plains with rosy hue;
Then in a wailful choir the small gnats mourn
  Among the river sallows, borne aloft
    Or sinking as the light wind lives or dies;
And full-grown lambs loud bleat from hilly bourn;
  Hedge-crickets sing; and now with treble soft
  The red-breast whistles from a garden croft;
    And gathering swallows twitter in the skies.

Bibliography

Allen, Glen O. "The Fall of Endymion: A Study in Keats's Intellectual Growth." *Keats-Shelley Journal,* 6 (1957), 37-57.

Allott, Miriam. " 'Isabella,' 'The Eve of St. Agnes,' and 'Lamia.' " In *John Keats: A Reassessment.* Ed. Kenneth Muir. Liverpool: Liverpool Univ. Press, 1958, pp. 40-63.

————. *Keats: The Complete Poems.* London: Longman, 1970.

Bate, W. J. *John Keats.* New York: Oxford Univ. Press, 1966.

Benvenuto, Richard. " 'The Ballance of Good and Evil' in Keats's Letters and in 'Lamia.' " *Journal of English and Germanic Philology,* 71 (1972), pp. 1-11.

Blackstone, Bernard. *The Consecrated Urn: An Interpretation of Keats in Terms of Growth and Form.* London: Longmans, 1959.

Bloom, Harold. *The Visionary Company.* Garden City, N. Y.: Doubleday, 1961.

Boulger, James. "Keats' Symbolism" *ELH,* 28 (1961), 244-59.

Brooks, Cleanth. "The Artistry of Keats: A Modern Tribute." In *The Major English Romantic Poets: A Symposium in Reappraisal.* Ed. C. D. Thrope, Carlos Baker, and Bennet Weaver. Carbondale: Southern Illinois Univ. Press, 1957, pp. 246-51.

Bush, Douglas. *Mythology and the Romantic Tradition in English Poetry.* New York: W.W. Norton, 1963.

Colvin, Sidney. *Keats.* London, 1887; rpt. London: Macmillan, 1957.

————. *John Keats: His Life and Poetry, His Friends, Critics, and After-Fame.* New York: Charles Scribner's Sons, 1917.

Evert, Walter. *Aesthetic and Myth in the Poetry of Keats.* Princeton: Princeton Univ. Press, 1965.

Fogle, R. H. "Keats's Ode to a Nightingale." *PMLA,* 68 (1953), 211-22.

Gittings, Robert. *John Keats.* Boston: Little, Brown, 1968.

Hughes, Merritt Y., ed. *John Milton: The Complete Poems and Major Prose.* New York: Odyssey Press, 1957.

Jones, James Land. *Adam's Dream: Mythic Consciousness in Keats and Yeats.* Athens, Ga.: Univ. of Georgia Press, 1975.

Lowes, J. L. *"Hyperion* and the *Purgatorio." Times Literary Supplement,* 11 Jan. 1936, p. 35.

Muir, Kenneth. "The Meaning of 'Hyperion.'" In *John Keats: A Reassessment.* Ed. Kenneth Muir. Liverpool: Liverpool Univ. Press, 1958, pp. 103-23.

Murry, John Middleton. *Keats.* New York: Noonday Press, 1955.

———. *Keats and Shakespeare.* London: Oxford Univ. Press, 1925.

Perkins, David. *The Quest for Permanence.* Cambridge, Mass.: Harvard Univ. Press, 1959.

Pettet, E. C. *On the Poetry of Keats.* Cambridge, Eng.: Cambridge Univ. Press, 1957.

Rollins, Hyder E., ed. *The Letters of John Keats, 1814-1821.* 2 vols. Cambridge, Mass.: Harvard Univ. Press, 1958.

Slote, Bernice. *Keats and the Dramatic Principle.* Lincoln, Neb.: Univ. of Nebraska Press, 1958.

Sperry, Stuart M. *Keats the Poet.* Princeton: Princeton Univ. Press, 1973.

———. "Richard Woodhouse's Interleaved and Annotated Copy of Keats's Poems (1817)." In *Literary Monographs 1.* Ed. E. Rothstein and T.K. Denseath. Madison: Univ. of Wisconsin Presss, 1967, pp. 103-164.

Stillinger, Jack. "The Hoodwinking of Madeline: Scepticism in 'The Eve of St. Agnes.'" *Studies in Philology,* 58 (1961), 533-55.

———, ed. *The Poems of John Keats.* Cambridge, Mass.: Harvard Univ. Press, 1978.

Van Ghent, Dorothy. "The Passion of the Groves." *Sewanee Review,* 52 (1944), 226-46.

Vendler, Helen. "The Experiential Beginnings of Keats's Odes." *Studies in Romanticism,* 12 (1973), pp. 591-606.

Ward, Aileen. *John Keats: The Making of a Poet.* New York: Viking Press, 1963.

Wasserman, Earl. *The Finer Tone: Keats's Major Poems.* Baltimore: Johns Hopkins Press, 1953.

Wicker, Brian. "The Disputed Lines in *The Fall of Hyperion." Essays in Criticism,* 7 (1957), 28-41.

Yeats, W.B. "At Stratford-on-Avon." In *Essays and Introductions.* New York: Macmillan, 1961, pp. 96-110.

Index